TOUHAMI ENNADRE

TOUHAMI

ENNADRE

BLACK LIGHT LUMIÈRE NOIRE SCHWARZES LICHT

With an essay by Avec un essai de Mit einem Beitrag von

FRANÇOIS AUBRAL

PRESTEL Munich · New York

This publication has been possible by grants from the Institut Français de Munich, AFAA (Ministère des Affaires Etrangères, Paris), represented by Bureau des Arts Plastiques, Cologne, Hypo-Kulturstiftung, Munich, and an anonymous donor.

Translation into German by Ingeborg Schmutte
Translation into English by Mark Hutchinson

Die Deutsche Bibliothek - CIP-Einheitsaufnahme
Ennadre, Touhami :
Black light – Lumière noire – Schwarzes Licht / Touhami Ennadre. With an essay by François Aubral. [Transl. into German by Ingeborg Schmutte. Transl. into Engl. by Mark Hutchinson]. – Munich · New York : Prestel, 1996
ISBN 3-7913-1735-0
NE: Aubral, François

Prestel-Verlag Mandlstraße 26 80802 Munich
Tel.: 089 3817090 Fax: 089 38170935

Edited by Peter Stepan and Christopher Wynne
Designed by Petra Lüer
Lithography by lithoservice Brodschelm, Munich
Printed by Passavia Druckerei GmbH, Passau
Bound by Buchbinderei Salzburg
Printed on acid-free paper
Printed in Germany

ISBN 3-7913-1735-0

BLACK LIGHT LUMIÈRE NOIRE SCHWARZES LICHT

"Works of art are born of those who confront danger, who go to the limit of an experience, to a point beyond which no human can go. The farther one ventures, the more distinctive, the more personal, the more unique a life becomes."

A shattering light. And a background darkness that's definitive. Birth, death, straight in the eyes now. Nerves, head and body. Remember: life. Violence is always despicable.

On seeing Touhami Ennadre's work for the first time, you will be sure to experience strong feelings. You will not remain indifferent, reserved, calm. Either you will flee, refusing to contemplate your image and the world, or you will be rooted to the spot, paralyzed yet forced to react when faced with the tragic side of existence. The shock that moves you is not that of an evil eye. It is not complacent about suffering, but labours to set you free. Its cathartic aim is quite simply shattering.

The most striking thing about Ennadre's work is its plastic unity, the necessity that runs through it. He starts out, he says, from the principle that "you must give. You must be truly true. It's heart-rending. It brings to the surface all kinds of things you're not familiar with. It's either that or nothing." He tries to find out "what's really real": "Light is what's really real, it's the only thing that obsesses me." He also claims not to know "what photography is". "I'm not a photographer. Technique isn't important, at most it's a means." The important thing lies elsewhere: to ward off "violence, misery and death". As is often the case when artists try to summarize what is at stake in their art, Ennadre's remarks are somewhat halting and contradictory, misleadingly so. To prevent the reader falling into a trap, therefore, we must show a little patience in unravelling some of the threads that "underlie the work" – threads composed of the artist's dreams and desires, his efforts to succeed, his labours and his life. "Threads that underlie the work": our use of metaphor suggests, perhaps, that we should begin at the beginning, even if everything in the end remains intertwined. Does the work we are examining, at each stage in its development, not seek to recover "first things", to restore the image of a buried past and manifest its presence?

In what universe did Ennadre first open his eyes? For a visual artist, the question is of more than anecdotal interest. Where did he first see light? He was born in Casablanca in Morocco in 1953, in a house in the medina, an old-fashioned working-class district where his mother made rugs. We should imagine, not a Moroccan villa, jealously concealing its patio, fountain and flowers, its pelmet arches or moucharabies from prying eyes, but a tiny house:

« Les œuvres d'art naissent toujours de qui affronte le danger, de qui est allé jusqu'au bout d'une expérience, jusqu'au point que nul humain ne peut dépasser. Plus loin on pousse et plus propre, plus personnelle, plus unique devient une vie. »

Eclats. Irruption de lumière sur noir définitif. Naissance, mort, droit dans vos yeux, nerfs, tête et corps. Rappelez-vous : la vie ... la violence est toujours odieuse.

Qui voit l'œuvre de Touhami Ennadre pour la première fois éprouve une sensation forte. Vous ne resterez pas indifférent, réservé, calme. Ou bien vous fuirez, refusant de regarder votre image et le monde, ou bien vous serez en arrêt, médusé et forcé de réagir devant le tragique de l'existence. La commotion qui vous émeut n'est pas porte-malheur, elle ne se complaît pas dans la souffrance, mais travaille à votre délivrance : sa finalité cathartique est éclatante.

Ce qui frappe devant cette œuvre est l'unité du projet plastique, la nécessité qui le traverse. Ennadre part, dit-il, du principe qu' « il faut donner. Il faut être vraiment vrai. Ça déchire. Ça amène un tas de choses que vous ne connaissez pas. C'est ça ou rien. » Il essaie de trouver le « réel le plus réel » : « la lumière est le réel du plus réel, c'est la seule chose qui m'obsède. » Il affirme aussi qu'il « ne sait pas ce que c'est que la photographie ». « Je ne suis pas photographe. La technique n'a aucune importance, c'est tout au plus un moyen. » L'essentiel est ailleurs : conjurer « la violence, la misère et la mort ». Afin que le lecteur ne se laisse pas piéger par ces propos, quelque peu heurtés et faussement contradictoires, comme en tiennent souvent les artistes qui cherchent à résumer ce qui est en jeu dans leur art, il importe que nous fassions montre d' un peu de patience pour démêler quelques-uns des fils de cet entrelacement de désir, de volonté, de rêve, de travail et de vie qui « sous-tendent l'œuvre ». « Fils », « entrelacement de fils qui sous-tendent l'œuvre ». Ce registre métaphorique vient-il nous suggérer de commencer par le commencement, même si tout, en définitive, demeure mêlé ? L'œuvre qui nous occupe ne s'efforce-t-elle pas en effet à chaque moment de son développement de retrouver l'originaire, de restaurer l'image d'un passé enseveli et d'en manifester la présence ? Ne puise-t-elle pas son énergie dans le passé au futur du présent ?

Dans quel univers Ennadre a-t-il ouvert les yeux ? A propos d'un artiste du visuel, la question dépasse largement l'anecdote. Où a-t-il vu sa première lumière ? Il est né en 1953, au Maroc, à Casablanca, dans une maison de la médina, vieux quartier traditionnel et populaire, où sa mère faisait des tapis. N'imaginons pas une villa

»Kunstdinge sind ja immer Ergebnisse des In-Gefahr-gewesen-Seins, des in einer Erfahrung Bis-ans-Ende-gegangen-Seins ... Je weiter man geht, desto eigener, desto persönlicher, desto einziger wird ja ein Erlebnis.«

Rainer Maria Rilke

Aufleuchten. Lichteinfall auf Tiefschwarz. Geburt, Tod, geradewegs in die Augen, in Nerven, Kopf und Körper. Vergessen wir nie: Leben ... Gewalt ist immer häßlich.

Wer das Werk von Touhami Ennadre zum ersten Mal sieht, wird tief berührt. Er kann nicht unbeteiligt, reserviert und gelassen bleiben. Entweder ergreift er die Flucht, weil er sich weigert, sein eigenes Bild und die Welt anzuschauen, oder er bleibt wie angewurzelt und muß unweigerlich angesichts der Tragik des Daseins reagieren. Die Erschütterung, die wir erfahren, ist kein schlechtes Omen, sie gefällt sich nicht im Schmerz, sondern arbeitet an unserer Befreiung: Ihre reinigende Wirkung wird offenbar.

Auffallend ist bei diesem Werk die Einheit der bildnerischen Konzeption, deren durchgängig zwingende Konsequenz. Ennadre geht, wie er sagt, von dem Grundsatz aus, daß »man geben muß. Man muß wahrhaft wahrhaftig sein. Das reißt einen innerlich entzwei. Das bringt Dinge ans Licht, von denen man selbst nichts weiß. Die Wahrheit oder nichts.« Er sucht »Wahrheit, das wahrhaftig Wahre« zu finden: »Das Licht ist das Wahrhaftigste, von ihm allein bin ich besessen.« Auch versichert er, daß er »nicht weiß, was Photographie ist.« »Ich bin kein Photograph. Die Technik ist bedeutungslos, bestenfalls ein Hilfsmittel.« Das Wesentliche liegt woanders, besteht darin, »Gewalt, Elend und Tod zu bannen«.

Um uns nicht in diesen etwas unvermittelten und teils scheinbar widersprüchlichen Äußerungen zu verfangen, wie sie Künstler oft zur Zusammenfassung dessen gebrauchen, was in ihrer Kunst auf dem Spiel steht, bedarf es einiger Geduld, bis sich einige der Fäden aus dem Knäuel von Wunsch, Wille, Traum, Arbeit und Leben herauslösen, die dem Werk ›zugrundeliegen‹. ›Fäden, die dem Werk zugrundeliegen‹: Sollte diese Metapher uns nahelegen, mit dem Anfang zu beginnen, selbst wenn letztlich alles verworren bleibt? Bemüht sich das Werk, mit dem wir uns befassen, nicht in jedem Augenblick seiner Entwicklung, das Ursprüngliche wiederzufinden, das Bild einer verhüllten Vergangenheit heraufzuholen und deren Gegenwart an den Tag zu legen? Holt es sich nicht seine Kraft aus der Vergangenheit für die Zukunft der Gegenwart?

In welcher Art Umfeld hat Ennadre das Licht der Welt erblickt? Da es sich um einen Künstler des Visuellen handelt, geht die Frage weit über das Anekdotische hinaus. Wo hat er sein erstes Licht

a few cramped rooms, no windows and a single veiled skylight in a corner. Darkness everywhere, sometimes lit up by a candle, and, as the only sign of light, a modest terrace under the roof, reserved for his mother's loom. His first encounter with light, then, and at the same time with art, was a rug, seen at very close range, the woolen threads crossing back and forth in time with his mother's hands and eyes. She was often pressed for time and would have to finish her work under the light of the stars, shimmering in the night. Ennadre's first plastic emotion, the archetype for his vision, was a maternal image focused on the only chinks of light to be salvaged from the darkness of the house.
He has never forgotten that primal image; it still punctuates his sense of time, and, print after print, he tries to resurrect it in all his photographs. Anyone familiar with the vitality of the crafts tradition as it still exists in Morocco to this day will understand that though, as Ennadre says, he never attended "art school, let alone photography school", his sensibility has been shaped by a very ancient culture.

When, as a child, he wanted to leave the private, indoor world of the home, only one possibility was open to him: the streets. Small, swarming streets where you must thread your way, winding in and out, sometimes in hand-to-hand combat, improvising unlikely routes in which the straight line is always the long way round. In thoroughfares like these, everything has to be conquered from one moment to the next. No path is ever marked, and if you lose your way you never get it back. You must adjust your speed, then, to changing circumstances, and when you want to get somewhere or obtain something, draw up a plan of action centred on that goal, take aim, concentrate, seal yourself off from your surroundings and, in a movement as precise as it is rapid, take hold on what you are seeking.
One can imagine the fate of children, their desires racked by poverty. How often, and well before the age of reason, Ennadre must have dreamed of stealing an orange: spotting it, seeing only the one that was within reach, blacking out the rest of the pile which must be sure not to collapse, surveying the watchful eyes of adults, making straight for the goal, quickly grabbing it on the sly, then taking shelter in the dark protective shadow of the mosque or his home, like a thief. Pure fiction, of course, which he makes up for today – at your expense and for your pleasure – with his Hasselblad.

Seeing an artist's work simply as the manifestation of its author's biography is the result of a grossly reductive aesthetic; it is nonetheless important to point up some of the high points of that life, for they inform the genesis and development of a creative force. With this in mind, we have just conjured up Ennadre's private background and early habits of mind, as well as the cognitive style and culture in which they are rooted. But since it is the work alone that interests us, let us abandon Ennadre's

marocaine cachant jalousement son patio, sa fontaine, ses fleurs, ses arcs à lambrequins ou ses moucharabiehs aux regards indiscrets, mais une toute petite maison : quelques pièces exiguës, pas de fenêtres, une seule lucarne voilée dans un recoin. Partout le noir, éclairé parfois d'une bougie, et, unique appel de lumière, une modeste terrasse sous le toit, réservée au métier à tisser de sa mère. Son premier rapport avec la lumière, et l'art tout à la fois, fut donc bien le tapis, vu de très près, où les fils de laine s'entrecroisaient au rythme des mains et des yeux de sa mère. Quand le temps pressait, il fallait souvent achever le travail à la lueur des étoiles, scintillantes dans la nuit. La première émotion plastique d'Ennadre, l'archétype de sa vision, fut une image maternelle focalisée sur les seuls points de lumière arrachés au noir de la maison. Il n'oubliera jamais cette image primitive qui rythme encore son temps et qu'il cherche à ressusciter, épreuve après épreuve, dans chacune de ses photographies. Qui connaît la vivacité de la tradition artisanale, aujourd'hui encore vivante dans un pays comme le Maroc, comprendra que, si, comme il le dit, Ennadre n'a fréquenté « aucune école d'art, et encore moins de photographie », la formation de sa sensibilité remonte loin dans une culture millénaire.

Lorsque, enfant, il souhaitait quitter le monde intérieur et privé de la maison, une seule solution s'offrait à lui : la rue. Ruelles grouillantes, où il faut serpenter, se faufiler, parfois au corps à corps, et improviser des trajectoires invraisemblables où la ligne droite est toujours le plus long chemin. Dans cet espace de circulation, tout est, à chaque instant, à conquérir. Aucun itinéraire n'impose son tracé, et qui perd sa place ne la retrouve pas. Donc, adapter sa vitesse à l'évolution des circonstances et lorsque l'on désire aboutir quelque part ou obtenir quelque chose, construire un plan d'approche centré sur son but, viser, se concentrer, faire le vide autour de soi et, dans un mouvement aussi précis que rapide, se saisir de ce que l'on recherche.
On imagine le sort des enfants, et leur envies tenaillées par la pauvreté. Combien de fois, bien avant l'âge de raison, Ennadre a-t-il dû rêver de voler une orange : la repérer, ne voir que celle qui était à sa portée, faire le noir sur le tas qui ne devait surtout pas s'écrouler, contrôler les regards vigilants des adultes, foncer au but, la saisir et à toute vitesse, en cachette, se réfugier dans l'ombre noire et protectrice de la mosquée, ou de la maison, comme un voleur. Pure fiction : trop bon fils et trop honnête, Ennadre n'a jamais volé d'orange. Il se rattrape aujourd'hui, à vos dépens, et pour votre plaisir, avec son Hasselblad.

Si voir dans une œuvre la simple manifestation sensible de la biographie de son auteur procède d'une esthétique lourdement réductrice, signaler quelques points forts de vie, fondateurs de la genèse et du développement de l'élan créateur,

gesehen? Er wurde 1953 in Marokko, in Casablanca, in einem Haus der Medina geboren, einem alten, traditionellen und volkstümlichen Viertel, dort, wo seine Mutter Teppiche webte. Nicht etwa in einer jener marokkanischen Villen, die ihren Patio, ihren Brunnen, ihre Blumen, ihre tropfsteinverzierten Hufeisenbögen oder ihre arabischen Balkone vor indiskreten Blicken sorgsam verbergen, sondern in einem ganz kleinen Haus mit einigen engen Räumen ohne Fenster, mit nur einer verhüllten Dachluke in einer Ecke. Überall das Schwarze, manchmal von einer Kerze beleuchtet, und als einziger Lichteinfall eine bescheidene Terrasse unter dem Dach, die dem Webstuhl der Mutter vorbehalten war. Sein erstes Verhältnis zum Licht und zugleich zur Kunst war denn auch der Teppich, aus nächster Nähe gesehen, an dem sich die Fäden im Rhythmus der Hände und Augen seiner Mutter ineinander verwoben. Wenn die Zeit drängte, mußte die Arbeit oft nachts bei funkelndem Sternenlicht vollendet werden. Die erste bildnerische Erschütterung Ennadres, Archetypus seiner Sehweise, war ein Bild der Mutter, nur auf die Lichtpunkte konzentriert, die dem Schwarz des Hauses entrissen waren. Niemals sollte er dieses einfache Bild vergessen, das immer noch den Rhythmus seines Tagesablaufs bestimmt und das er, ein um das andere Mal, in jeder seiner Photographien zum Leben zu erwecken sucht. Wer weiß, wie lebendig die Handwerkstradition ist, die noch heute in einem Land wie Marokko weiterlebt, wird verstehen, daß die Schulung seiner Sensibilität weit zurückreicht in eine tausendjährige Kultur, denn Ennadre hat, wie er selbst sagt, »keine Kunstschule, geschweige denn eine Schule der Photographie« besucht.

Wenn er als Kind die innere und private Welt des Hauses verlassen wollte, gab es nur eins für ihn: die Straße. Ein Sträßchengewimmel, worin man sich schlängeln, sich manchmal Körper an Körper hindurchwinden und unwahrscheinliche Wegverläufe improvisieren mußte, wo die gerade Linie stets der weiteste Weg war. In diesem Lebensbereich muß alles in jedem Augenblick erobert werden. Keine Wegstrecke ist in ihrem Verlauf eindeutig, und wer seinen Platz verliert, findet ihn nicht wieder. Es gilt folglich, sein Tempo der Entwicklung der Umstände anzupassen und wenn man an einem Ort ankommen oder etwas erreichen möchte, muß man einen Annäherungsplan auf sein Ziel entwerfen, es anpeilen, sich konzentrieren, sich Freiraum verschaffen und mit einer ebenso genauen wie schnellen Bewegung sich dessen bemächtigen, wonach man trachtet. Man kann sich das Schicksal der Kinder, ihre von der Armut geknebelten Gelüste vorstellen. Wie oft mag Ennadre – lange bevor er im urteilsfähigen Alter war – davon geträumt haben, eine Orange zu stehlen: Sie aussuchen, nur die eine in seiner Reichweite, den Haufen schwarz ausblenden, der vor allem nicht einstürzen durfte, die wachsamen Blicke der Erwachsenen im Auge behalten, auf das Ziel losschnellen, sie packen und sich in Windeseile, ungesehen, wie ein Dieb, in den schwarzen schützenden Schatten der Moschee oder des Hauses flüchten. Reine Erfindung: Ennadre

childhood and turn to the moment when he first held a camera in his hands. It was in Paris in 1975. His father, a butcher from the heart of the medina, had come seeking work at a foundry in the Paris suburbs, where he would later go blind. Ennadre, who "had never seen snow", was only seven when the great voyage took place, uprooting and transplanting him, and making him, much later, an inhabitant of Paris and, in 1986, a French citizen. He knew only the Arab spoken in the medina, so a French school taught him, as best it could, to write French. Immigrating into another language in this way involved many labour pains and was carried out on the margins of society. How, in a situation such as this, with the eclipse of one's mother tongue and the difficult birth of a second language, can one adequately express the effects of violence occasioned by one's new life, characteristic of an entire generation of North Africans? Ennadre did what they all did: he "slaved away", putting all his strength and hopes into soccer. If Ennadre himself is to be believed, it was practising this sport which gave him his real education in street-life and fighting; he saw it as the only way of escaping, of being among friends and drawing up an offensive strategy that would arm him against the violence of life. Football, which he had been playing ever since the medina in Casablanca, "taught him everything", in particular a way of looking at things that he would later make use of in photography. He only shoots, only activates his camera – dribbling first, feigning if need be – when the moment is right, so that one only really sees the goal once the ball is in the net. As it turns out, Ennadre has not become a professional footballer, much to his regret: he only takes photographs to fulfill his teenage dream. This hiccup in his career is cause, surely, for celebration!

At the same time, things were going from bad to worse, and his mother, after presenting him with an electric organ which he had to give up because it woke his father up, thought of buying him a camera. Why? To keep her son busy, to keep him out of harm's way, to channel his energies, certainly.

But something more profound had occured, for nothing at the time destined him for photography, not the slightest conscious desire. His mother, it must be said, had just begun showing the first symptoms of the illness that would kill her. "Is there a desire to pass life on", wonders Ennadre, "in someone who knows they're going to die?" By way of response, let us note that he used his first camera to take photographs of his mother and her friends. This woman, though only aware of it in mysterious ways, forever after associated her agony and dying with her son's first photographic endeavours. The death he had just experienced inwardly for the first time, this death that "engulfed" and "shattered" him, "toppling [him] into solitude", became his twin sister, his accomplice in the birth of photography. Today, he still remembers this every time he approaches a camera, a negative or a sheet of photographic paper: "I've always been escorted by my past, my loneliness and what I've lived through. It's idiotic, but I can never talk about my work without talking about my mother, because I come

s'impose. Dans cet esprit, nous venons d'évoquer l'espace subjectif et les habitudes mentales originaires d'Ennadre, ainsi que le style cognitif et la culture où ils s'enracinent. Mais, l'œuvre seule nous intéressant, abandonnons Ennadre à son enfance et retrouvons-le au moment où il a pour la première fois un appareil photographique dans les mains. C'était à Paris, en 1975. Entre-temps, son père, boucher au cœur de la médina, était venu chercher du travail dans une fonderie de la banlieue parisienne où il perdra les yeux.

Ennadre n'avait que sept ans quand intervint, pour lui qui « n'avait jamais vu la neige », le grand voyage, l'arrachement, la transplantation qui en fera, bien plus tard, un habitant de Paris et, en 1986, un citoyen de nationalité française. Ne sachant de l'arabe que ce que l'on en parlait à la médina, l'école communale française l'initia, tant bien que mal, à écrire le français. Cette immigration dans une autre langue s'opéra avec douleur, et à la marge de la société. Comment, en situation d'éclipse de la langue maternelle et d'accouchement difficile de la langue d'adoption, exprimer à leur juste mesure les effets de violence de sa nouvelle vie, propres à toute une génération d'Africains du Nord ? Ennadre fit comme les autres : il « galéra » et mobilisa sa force vitale et ses espoirs dans le football. Si on l'en croit, c'est la pratique de ce sport qui a constitué sa véritable culture, dans la rue et le combat ; il y a vu la seule façon de s'en sortir, d'être entre amis et de se constituer une tactique et une stratégie offensive capable de l'armer contre les violences de la vie. Le « foot », qu'il pratiquait déjà dans la médina de Casablanca, lui a « tout appris », notamment le type de regard qu'il exploitera ultérieurement en photographie. Il ne shoote, ne déclenche son appareil, qu'après avoir driblé, rusé s'il le faut, au moment juste pour que l'on ne voit vraiment le but que lorsque le ballon est dans le filet. La vie a fait qu'Ennadre n'est pas devenu footballeur professionnel, c'est son grand regret : il ne photographie que pour réaliser son rêve de jeunesse : réjouissons-nous de cet incident de carrière !

Les problèmes allant néanmoins croissant, sa mère, après lui avoir offert un orgue électrique auquel il dut renoncer parce qu'il réveillait son père, eut l'idée de lui procurer un appareil photographique. Pourquoi ? Occuper son fils, le détourner des dangers, canaliser son énergie, certes. Mais quelque chose de plus profond venait de se passer, car rien ne le destinait alors à la photographie, pas la moindre envie consciente. Il faut dire qu'à ce moment-là, sa mère venait de ressentir les premiers symptômes de la maladie qui allait la foudroyer. « Existe-t-il, se demande Ennadre, chez quelqu'un qui sait qu'il va mourir, le désir de se transmettre ? » Pour seule réponse, constatons qu'avec ce premier appareil il prit des photographies de sa mère et de ses amies. Cette femme, ne le sachant que mystérieusement, associa définitivement son agonie et sa mort aux premières tentatives photographiques de son fils. La mort qu'il venait de vivre de l'intérieur pour la première fois, cette mort qui l'a « englouti », « effondré » et « fait

hat als viel zu guter, zu ehrlicher Sohn nie Orangen gestohlen. Heute holt er das mit seiner Hasselblad nach, auf unsere Kosten und zu unserem Vergnügen.

In einem Werk einfach nur den spürbaren Ausdruck der Biographie seines Autors zu sehen, heißt, von einer plump reduzierten Ästhetik auszugehen; andererseits kann man nicht umhin, einige starke Momente des Lebens zu benennen, die Ursprung und Entwicklung des Schöpferischen begründen. In diesem Sinn haben wir eine Vorstellung von Lebensgefühl und Denkweise des jungen Ennadre gewonnen sowie von der Geisteshaltung und Kultur, in der sie beheimatet sind. Da uns jedoch allein das Werk interessiert, verlassen wir den Jugendlichen und treffen ihn in dem Moment wieder, als er zum ersten Mal einen Photoapparat in Händen hält: Das ist 1975 in Paris. In der Zwischenzeit war sein Vater, zuvor Metzger in der Medina, auf der Suche nach Arbeit in die Gießerei eines Pariser Vororts gekommen (wo er später das Augenlicht einbüßen sollte). Ennadre war erst sieben Jahre alt, als für ihn, der »niemals Schnee gesehen hatte«, die große Reise begann, die ihn herausriß, verpflanzte und sehr viel später, 1986, zu einem Einwohner von Paris, einem Bürger französischer Nationalität werden ließ. Das Arabische kannte er nur, wie man es in der Medina sprach. Die französische Grundschule vermittelte ihm schlecht und recht die französische Schriftsprache. Diese Einwanderung in eine andere Sprache geschah unter Schmerzen, am Rande der Gesellschaft. Wie sollte er, dem die Muttersprache verlorenging und der eine Adoptivsprache mühsam lernen mußte, die Gewalterfahrungen in seinem neuen Leben angemessen ausdrücken, wie sie eine ganze Generation von Nordafrikanern macht? Ennadre erlebte wie die anderen die Not und setzte seine körperliche Kraft und seine Hoffnungen beim Fußball ein. Wenn man ihm glauben darf, hat er auf der Straße und im Kampf bei diesem Sport seine eigentliche Bildung erhalten. Er sah seine einzige Überlebenschance darin, unter Freunden zu sein und eine offensive Taktik und Strategie für sich auszubilden, um sich gegen die Gewalttätigkeiten des Lebens zu wappnen. Bereits in der Medina von Casablanca hatte er Fußball gespielt, der ihm »alles beigebracht« hat, insbesondere die Art des Blicks, den er später in der Photographie nutzen sollte. Erst nach dem Dribbeln, wenn nötig nach Täuschungsmanövern schießt er, drückt er im richtigen Augenblick ab, damit das Ziel erst dann wirklich erkannt wird, wenn der Ball bereits im Netz ist. Ennadres Leben hat einen Verlauf genommen, der ihn zu seinem Leidwesen nicht zum professionellen Fußballspieler gemacht hat. Er photographiert nur, um sich seinen Jugendtraum zu erfüllen: Freuen wir uns über diese Wendung in seiner Laufbahn!

Als weitere Probleme hinzukamen, schenkte ihm seine Mutter eine elektrische Orgel, auf die er allerdings wieder verzichten mußte, weil er seinen Vater damit im Schlaf störte. So kam sie auf die Idee, ihm einen Photoapparat zu schenken. Warum? Vermutlich wollte sie ihren Sohn beschäftigen, Gefahren von ihm abwenden, seine Energie lenken. Es war jedoch noch etwas Tiefergehendes geschehen, denn, was Touhami betrifft, zog ihn zu der Zeit nichts, nicht der geringste bewußte Wunsch zur Photographie. Man muß wissen, daß seine Mutter

from someone. I was a witness to her life, and my work is simply a kind of witness to this person I once knew. Obviously, you can't understand that; it's like my work, you really have to live with it. People want to understand what I'm doing immediately, but you can't enter into my work immediately. It took me years to do it myself."

Photographs of the family circle, brief images of the suburbs: Moroccans, Portugese, Yugoslavians slitting the throats of pigs. The first outside photograph he took was in London: a tramp with his bottle, trying to catch a pigeon, like Ennadre trying to capture his image with his lens, coming as close as possible. An on-the-job apprenticeship, with no teachers and no technical training. Trial and error, improvisation, pottering about: we can assume that he knew nothing, and still knows nothing probably, of the basic notions of photography set out in a manual for beginners. No matter! He put them all together in his own way, out of necessity and circumstance. He forged, not a technique, which would have to be something you could pass on, but a personal approach formed from one failure after another, unintentional misfocusings, botched negatives and disastrous prints that he would throw away or lose.

Remote from theoretical notions and the traditional rules of photography, he created a protocol that is part and parcel of his vision and ruled by his one "obsession", light. I know of only one photography "teacher" as far as Ennadre is concerned. The lesson was unique and lasted less than three seconds. Nevertheless, he owes a great deal to that teacher. Let us call him the "teacher despite himself", or the "teacher who broke in". One day, while developing some still-born negatives in a makeshift lab, someone – he doesn't know who – opened the door by mistake and apologized. Light entered, blackening the paper. Ennadre had just been introduced to light in photography, his own. He would never forget. And work to be done again, with no regard for convention and prejudice.

Between these first faltering endeavours and the departure for Asia that would result in his first exhibited work, *Hands, back, feet,* two voyages deserve a moment's pause. The first was Casablanca, where he went to bury his mother. He wanted to photograph the agony of separation, the boundless pain he felt watching his aunt hugging one of his sisters. He "couldn't" – nor, I would add, did he wish nor need to – "photograph their faces": he photographed his aunt's hands "at very close range", hands which in themselves embodied all the weight of the family's pain.

Next came a detour to New York. In the house where he was staying he had access to a large library specialized in the history of photography. He looked at everything, rapidly and in no particular order, and realized that he should continue – or, rather, decided he should begin – taking photography seriously as a "medium". He marvelled at the pioneers who worked with very

basculer dans la solitude», devenait sœur jumelle et complice de la naissance de la photographie en lui. Cela, il se le rappelle aujourd'hui, encore et toujours, toutes les fois qu'il approche un appareil, un négatif ou du papier: «J'ai toujours été escorté par mon passé, ma solitude et ce que j'ai vécu. C'est idiot, mais je ne peux jamais parler de mon travail sans parler de ma mère, parce que je viens de quelqu'un. J'ai été témoin de sa vie, et mon œuvre n'est qu'une espèce de témoignage de cette personne que j'ai connue. Evidemment, vous ne pouvez comprendre ; c'est comme mon travail, il faut vraiment vivre avec. Les gens veulent comprendre tout de suite ce que je fais, mais on ne peut rentrer tout de suite dans mon travail. Moi, ça m'a pris des années.»

Photographie du cercle de famille, images brèves de banlieue: Marocains, Portugais, et Yougoslaves qui égorgent des cochons. La première photographie extérieure fut prise à Londres: un clochard, avec sa bouteille, essayant d'attraper un pigeon, comme Ennadre, avec son objectif, tentant d'attraper son image, en se rapprochant le plus possible. Apprentissage sur le tas, sans maîtres ni connaissances techniques. Tâtonnements, improvisations, bricolage: gageons qu'il ignorait tout, comme aujourd'hui probablement encore, des notions de base exposées dans un manuel élémentaire de photographie. Qu'importe ! Il a reconstruit tout cela à sa mesure, au gré des nécessités, des circonstances. Il s'est forgé non pas une technique, qui, en tant que telle, devrait être transmissible, mais une approche personnelle, faite de ratages successifs, de flous non désirés, de négatifs bousillés et d'épreuves catastrophes qu'il jeta, qu'il perdit. Loin de toute assimilation des notions théoriques et des règles du jeu classique, il créa un protocole photographique inhérent à sa vision et régi par sa seule «obsession» de la lumière. A titre d'exemple, je ne lui connais qu'un «professeur» de photographie. La leçon fut unique et ne dura pas trois secondes. Il lui doit cependant beaucoup. Appelons-le, le «professeur-malgré lui» ou le «professeur par effraction». Un jour, alors qu'il développait, avec des moyens de fortune, dans un labo improvisé, des négatifs morts-nés, il ne sait qui, par inadvertance, ouvrit la porte et s'excusa. La lumière entra, noircissant les papiers. Ennadre venait de faire connaissance avec la lumière en photographie, la sienne. Il n'oubliera pas. Rideau, et travail à refaire, par-delà conventions et préjugés.

Entre ces balbutiements et son départ pour l'Asie d'où il ramena son premier travail exposé: *Les Mains, le dos, les pieds*, deux voyages méritent un temps d'arrêt. Casablanca d'abord, où il se rendit pour enterrer sa mère. Il voulut photographier son déchirement, l'infini de sa douleur, qu'il vit en regardant sa tante qui enlaçait l'une de ses sœurs. Il ne «pouvait», j'ajoute: il ne voulait ni ne devait, «prendre leurs visages»: il photographia les mains de sa tante «de très près», ces mains qui incarnaient à elles seules le poids de la douleur de la famille.

gerade damals die ersten Anzeichen der Krankheit verspürte, an der sie bald sterben sollte. »Gibt es bei dem, der weiß, daß er sterben wird, den Wunsch, sich weiterzugeben?« fragt sich Ennadre. Wir können eine Antwort nur darin sehen, daß er mit diesem ersten Photoapparat Aufnahmen von seiner Mutter und den Freundinnen machte. Diese Frau stellte in geheimnisvoller Vorahnung zwischen ihrem Siechtum, ihrem Tod und den ersten photographischen Versuchen ihres Sohnes eine Verbindung her. Der Tod, den er zum ersten Mal tief in sich erlebte, dieser Tod, der ihn »verschlungen«, »niedergeschmettert« und »in Einsamkeit aus dem Gleichgewicht« gebracht hat, wurde für ihn zum Zwillingsbruder und Helfer bei der Entstehung seiner Photographie. Daran erinnert er sich heute stets aufs neue, jedesmal, wenn er zu einem Photoapparat, einem Negativ oder zum Papier greift: »Meine Vergangenheit, meine Einsamkeit und alles, was ich durchgemacht habe, sind meine ständigen Leibwächter. Es ist dumm, aber ich kann von meiner Arbeit nicht sprechen, ohne von meiner Mutter zu sprechen, weil ich von jemandem abstamme. Ich war Zeuge ihres Lebens, und mein Werk legt in gewisser Weise Zeugnis von dieser Person ab, die ich gekannt habe. Es ist schwer nachvollziehbar, aber es ist wie meine Arbeit, man muß wirklich mit ihr leben. Die Leute wollen sofort verstehen, was ich mache, aber man kann nicht sofort in meine Arbeit einsteigen. Ich selbst habe immerhin Jahre dazu gebraucht.«

Familienphotos, knappe Bildfolgen aus den Vorortvierteln: Marokkaner, Portugiesen und Jugoslawen, wie sie Schweine schlachten. Das erste Straßenbild nahm er in London auf: einen Clochard mit seiner Flasche, der eine Taube einzufangen versucht, vergleichbar Ennadre, wie er so nah wie möglich heranzugehen versucht, um mit seinem Objektiv ein Bild zu erhaschen. Lehrzeit vor Ort, ohne Lehrer und ohne technische Kenntnisse. Erste Versuche, Improvisationen, Bastelarbeiten: Man könnte wetten, daß er – wie wahrscheinlich auch heute noch – nichts von den Grundbegriffen wußte, die in einem Lehrbuch der Photographie stehen. Was macht's! Er hat alles, wie er es brauchte und die Umstände es erforderten, neu geschaffen. Er hat für sich keine Technik ertüftelt, die als solche übertragbar sein müßte, sondern aus verschiedenen Fehlerfahrungen, unerwünschten Unschärfen, verdorbenen Negativen und verfehlten Abzügen, die er wegwarf, die er verlor, sich einen eigenen Zugang erarbeitet. Ohne sich die theoretischen Begriffe und die klassischen Regeln anzueignen, hat er Photographien protokollarisch festgehalten, wie sie in seiner Vision entstanden und allein von seiner ›Besessenheit‹ vom Licht gelenkt wurden. Ich weiß bei ihm nur um einen ›Lehrer‹ der Photographie. Es gab nur eine einmalige Lektion, kaum drei Sekunden lang. Und doch verdankt er ihr viel. Wir wollen ihn den ›Lehrer wider Willen‹ oder den ›Einbruchlehrer‹ nennen. Als Ennadre eines Tages mit zufälligen Mitteln in einem improvisierten Labor mißlungene Negative entwickelte, öffnete jemand achtlos die Tür und entschuldigte sich. Licht drang ein und schwärzte die Papiere. Ennadre machte die Bekanntschaft mit dem Licht in der Photographie, seinem Licht. Er sollte es nicht vergessen, zog einen Schlußstrich und begann neu mit der Arbeit, jenseits von Konventionen und Vorurteilen.

large plates and negatives and established a new relationship to light, but came to feel that the history of photography was not for him. The studio portrait, the cosy family scene, the social survey, soft-focus photography, landscapes, all forms of photo-journalism and documentary, fashion, postcard and art photography, photo-montage, the "chic-shock" clichés of advertising and the rest, the great tradition of the snapshot – none of these things really meant anything to him. Reason enough for him to prefer not to talk about it and – elsewhere, somewhere apart, in his own particular way – stick to his own path. Explaining why Ennadre feels no great affinities with the heroes of contemporary photography is of little interest for anyone trying to understand the particular logic of his work. Once he is more familiar with it, the reader will come to understand for himself why Ennadre does not see himself as a photographer, seeking instead, he tells us, what "cannot be photographed". To avoid talking at cross-purposes or arguing about schools, let us confront the images themselves and the process of creation that underlies them as threads underlie the beauty of a rug.

Shooting, developing, selecting contact-plates, analyzing working proofs and printing in large formats constitute one and the same act, which must be understood as a whole. Ennadre performs each of these operations himself, integrating them in an overall approach that confers a unity upon them. "In the beginning was action", says Faust. Ennadre explains: "My eye takes priority over the view-finder. The viewfinder is like a keyhole: you can see what the others are doing, but you're not in the action. To be in the action, I took the viewfinder off my Hasselblad".

Removing the viewfinder brought him a twofold freedom: that of the eyes, which focus directly on the area to be reflected on the negative, and that of the hands, which adjust the lens in directions variable up to infinity in order to decide the best angle. The camera is put in its place, that of an eye that follows the movements of the photographer's hands in pursuit of the figure he is seeking, abandoning itself to a kind of ritual dance around and, as it were, within the scene in question, in search of that "clear, focused moment" when the lens approaches the subject "at very close range" and the shutter is released. "Objects in relief viewed at close range, through a single eye, will produce the effect of a perfect picture", wrote Leonardo da Vinci. With a camera you need to have "a view-finder in your head", to be "your own rangefinder", and to have an intuitive knowledge of framing that only comes after years of trial and error.

This technical bias suggests that Ennadre's forging of a personal photographic style is linked to his use of a lens with a constant focal length: a wide-angle lens, exclusively; and used, moreover, at extremely close quarters. A wide-angle lens, not to enlarge the field of vision, but in order to "come in close". Enough to make the purists shudder. Using a type of focal length designed for architecture in a contrary and unnatural manner allows Ennadre to create his

Un détour par New York ensuite. Il y fut hébergé dans une maison où il eut accès à une importante bibliothèque spécialisée dans l'histoire de la photographie. Il regarda tout, très vite, dans le désordre, et comprit qu'il devait continuer ou, plutôt, décida de commencer à prendre le «moyen» photographique au sérieux. Il fut émerveillé par les pionniers de la photographie qui travaillaient sur des plaques, des négatifs très grands, et établissaient un rapport nouveau avec la lumière. Mais après, il sentit que l'histoire de la photographie n'était pas sa tasse de thé à la menthe. Le portrait posé, l'intimisme familial, l'enquête sociale, les scènes d'ambiance, le paysage, toutes les formes de reportages et de documentaires, la mode, la photographie esthétisante, la photographie d'art, les photo-montages, les clichés choc et chic de la pub et le reste, la grande tradition de l'instantané, rien de tout cela ne lui parlait vraiment. La raison est suffisante pour préférer qu'il n'en parle pas et à côté, ailleurs, à sa manière, poursuive son chemin. Expliquer pourquoi Ennadre éprouve peu d'affinités avec les héros de la photographie contemporaine ne présente qu'un faible intérêt pour qui s'interroge sur la logique spécifique de son œuvre. Quand le lecteur sera plus familier avec elle, il comprendra de lui-même pourquoi Ennadre ne se considère pas comme photo-graphe, mais dit rechercher ce qui «n'est pas photographiable». Evitons controverses d'écoles et malentendus et confrontons-nous aux images, au processus de création qui les sous-tend, comme les fils sous-tendent la beauté du tapis.

Prise de vue, développement, sélection sur planches-contact, analyse des épreuves de travail et grand tirage ne forment qu'un seul et même acte, que l'on doit appréhender comme une totalité. Ennadre effectue lui-même chacune de ces opérations interdépendantes et les intègre dans une démarche qui leur confère une unité. «Au commencement était l'action», disait Faust. Ennadre s'explique: «Je fais passer mon œil avant le viseur. Le viseur, c'est comme un trou de serrure: on voit ce que les autre font, mais on n'est pas dans l'action. Pour être dans l'action, j'ai enlevé le viseur de mon Hasselblad.» Cette privation de viseur lui apporte une double liberté: celle des yeux, qui regardent directement la section d'espace à réfléchir sur le négatif, et celle des mains, qui orientent l'objectif, selon des directions variables à l'infini, pour décider du meilleur angle. L'appareil est remis à sa place, celle d'un œil que les gestes du photographe déplacent au gré de la figure recherchée, se livrant, autour et, pour ainsi dire, à l'intérieur de la scène, à une sorte de danse rituelle, en quête du «moment clair et net» où, «approchant de très près» l'objectif du sujet, il déclenche. «Les objets en relief vus de tout près, d'un seul œil, produiront l'effet d'un tableau parfait», écrivait Léonard de Vinci. Encore convient-il, avec un appareil photographique, d'avoir «le viseur dans la tête», d'être «son propre télémètre» et de disposer d'une connaissance intuitive du cadrage, fruit de nombreuses années d'essais et de travail. Un tel parti-pris laisse entendre qu'Ennadre s'est forgé une perception photographique propre, liée à l'utilisation d'un objectif à focale constante:

Zwischen diesen frühesten Anfängen und seiner Reise nach Asien, von der er seine ersten Ausstel-lungsarbeiten mitbrachte – *Hände, Rücken, Füße* –, verdienen zwei Reisen Beachtung. Zunächst die nach Casablanca, wohin er zur Beerdigung seiner Mutter fuhr. Er wollte seinen tiefen Schmerz photo-graphieren, wie er es beim Anblick seiner Tante wahrnahm, als sie eine seiner Schwestern umarmte. Er ›konnte‹ nicht, ich füge hinzu, er wollte und sollte ihre Gesichter nicht ›aufnehmen‹: Er photo-graphierte aus größter Nähe die Hände seiner Tante, diese Hände, die für sich allein schon die Schwere des Leids der Familie verkörperten.

Dann ein Umweg über New York. Dort fand er Aufnahme in einem Haus, das ihm Zugang zu einer großen Spezialbibliothek über die Geschichte der Photographie gewährte. Er schaute sich alles plan-los und zügig an und begriff, daß er weitermachen mußte, oder, besser gesagt, er beschloß, das ›Mit-tel‹ Photographie von nun an ernstzunehmen. Zwar war er erstaunt zu entdecken, wie die Pioniere der Photographie sehr große Negative auf Platten bear-beitet und ein neues Verhältnis zum Licht hergestellt hatten. Doch merkte er später, daß die Geschichte der Photographie nicht seine Tasse Pfefferminztee war. Das gestellte Porträt, die private Familien-sphäre, die Sozialstudie, Stimmungsszenen, Landschaften, alle Formen der Reportage, der Dokumentation, Mode, Schönheits- und Kunstpho-tos, Photomontagen, Schick- und Schockklischees der Werbung und ähnliches, die lange Tradition der Schnappschüsse, nichts von alledem sprach ihn wirklich an. Es gibt genügend Gründe dafür, daß er darüber nicht spricht und seinen Weg auf seine Weise weiterverfolgt. Wer nach der besonderen Logik in seinem Werk fragt, den wird es kaum ver-wundern, daß Ennadre wenig Beziehung zu den Helden der zeitgenössischen Photographie hat. Wer vertrauter mit seinem Werk ist, wird erkennen, warum Ennadre sich nicht als Photograph versteht, warum er sagt, er suche das, was »nicht photogra-phierbar« ist. Wir wollen Kontroversen zwischen Schulen und Mißverständnisse aussparen und uns mit den Bildern, dem Schöpfungsprozeß befassen, der ihnen wie die Fäden der Schönheit eines Teppichs zugrundeliegt. Photoaufnahme, Entwick-lung, Auswahl auf Kontaktabzügen, Prüfung der Probeabzüge und Vergrößerung bilden einen Vor-gang, den man als Einheit verstehen muß. Ennadre nimmt selbst jede dieser voneinander abhängigen Handlungen vor und bringt sie in einen Zusammen-hang, der sie zu einer Einheit verbindet. »Am Anfang war die Tat«, sagte Faust. Ennadre erklärt über sich: »Ich schaue mit bloßem Auge, statt in den Sucher zu sehen. Der Sucher ist wie ein Schlüs-selloch: Man sieht, was die anderen machen, ist aber nicht im Geschehen. Um im Geschehen zu sein, habe ich den Sucher meiner Hasselblad ent-fernt.« Der fehlende Sucher macht ihn zweifach frei: mit den Augen, die den auszumachenden Aus-schnitt, den das Negativ wiedergeben soll, unmittel-bar sehen, und mit den Händen, die das Objektiv in unendlich veränderbare Stellung bringen, um den besten Winkel herauszufinden. Der Apparat tritt an die Stelle des Auges, folgt den Bewegungen des Photographen zum gesuchten Objekt hin. Die-ser begibt sich rund um die Szene und gewisser-maßen in sie hinein, in einer Art rituellem Tanz, auf der Suche nach dem »lichten und scharfen

image and, at this stage of his labours, to considerably flatten out effects of depth and perspective. This is only possible because a photograph, when treated in this way, will attain its definitive state only during enlargement, at which point Ennadre, as we shall see, himself imposes relief and light. A wide-angle lens, on account of the direction given to the centre line of sight, introduces a slight distortion which, when controlled, helps form the negative image. It is hard to see how such a method of shooting would allow one to establish the traditional measures and settings: life is too short to waste time changing lenses and turning rings. In order to remain in focus, then, the camera is permanently immobilized at maximum speed and middle stop. But, one might object, how is one to ensure there is enough light in all circumstances? Ennadre responds by fitting out his camera, on top and bottom, with two electric torches whose light converges at the intersection of the centre of the subject and the lens's centre line of sight. Day or night, he works with his own light, which is always the same and is necessarily gov-erned by the position of the lens. This allows him to obliterate shadows, the centre line of sight being perpendicular to the subject; or, alternatively, to turn them to his own advantage by deliberately accentuating them, playing on the position that the luminous eye, the camera, occupies in space.

When developing his films, Ennadre takes into account the circumstances under which the shots were taken, so that he ends up with films and contact-plates whose format (6 x 6 cm) is too small for the next stage of his work. Having first made a selection, then, he prints a series of working proofs (24 x 30 cm) which he analyzes and evaluates before making a further selection. These are not finished works, merely flat prints on paper with no relief and no real light, in which the effect of perspective has been suppressed – rough copies, sketches, embryonic forms of works which have not yet come to light. On examination most of these proofs will be abandoned; the choice is draconian. At this stage, Ennadre will sometimes arrange his images in pairs or triptychs. It is now, for the elect, that the great labour begins. Once again, he distances himself from traditional photography: whereas any conscientious lab assistant, provided he follows the instructions he has been given, can make a print, in Ennadre's work time intervenes forcefully between the different operations, above all during enlargement. This time factor has more in common with that of the plastic arts than with the instantaneous time of photography.

But let us return to the negative Ennadre has selected. It takes the form of a potential work that has not yet been actualized; what it lacks is light. It is a kind of virtual image from which the eye and hand of the artist will help deliver the image proper. Here, Ennadre's manner is a child of those Renaissance painters who sought to determine the outline of a figure, its "silhouette", its "composition" and, finally, the "reception of light", according to the terms used by Alberti in his *De Pictura* (1435). The first act is to draw the figure's outline at the centre of the image with the aid of a mask designed

le grand angle, et lui seul, opérant, qui plus est, de façon extrêmement rapprochée. Grand angle, non pas pour élargir le champ de vision, mais pour « s'approcher ». De quoi faire frémir les puristes. En usant en sens inverse et contre-nature de ce type de focale destinée à l'architecture, Ennadre forme son image et, à ce stade de son travail, aplatit considérablement l'effet de profondeur et de perspective. Ce n'est possible que parce que la photographie ainsi traitée n'atteindra son état définitif que lors de l'agrandissement où, nous le verrons, Ennadre lui impose relief et lumière. Le grand angle, en fonction de la direction donnée au rayon central, induit une légère distorsion qui, contrôlée, contribue à former l'image négative. On voit mal comment un tel protocole de prise de vue permettrait d'établir les mesures et les réglages traditionnels : la vie va trop vite pour que l'on perde son temps à changer les objectifs et à en tourner les bagues. Il en résulte que l'appareil est définitivement immobilisé sur la vitesse maximale et sur un diaphragme moyen, pour la netteté. Mais objectera-t-on, comment avoir assez de lumière en toutes circonstances ? Ennadre répond en harnachant son appareil, en haut et en bas, de deux torches électroniques dont les lumières convergent au point d'intersection entre le centre du sujet et le rayon central de l'objectif. Qu'il fasse jour ou nuit, il travaille avec sa lumière, toujours la même, et nécessairement orientée par la position de l'objectif, ce qui lui permet d'anéantir les ombres, le rayon central étant perpendiculaire au sujet, ou d'en tirer partie en les accentuant à dessein, jouant alors sur la position de l'œil lumineux dans l'espace, l'appareil.

Ennadre développe ses pellicules en tenant compte des circonstances de sa prise de vue; il obtient des films et des planches-contact d'un format (6 x 6 cm) trop petit pour la suite de son travail. Aussi, après une première sélection, tire-t-il en série des épreuves de travail (24 x 30 cm) afin de les analyser, évaluer et sélectionner. Il ne s'agit pas d'œuvres, mais de simples tirages sur papier, plats, sans relief ni réelle lumière, où l'effet de perspective est écrasé. Brouillons, esquisses, forme embryonnaire de l'œuvre qui n'est pas encore née à la lumière. Après examen, la plupart de ces épreuves seront abandonnées : le choix est draconien. Dès ce moment, Ennadre constitue parfois des paires et des triptyques. Et, pour les élus, le grand travail commence. Il prend ici encore ses distances avec la photographie traditionnelle où un laborantin consciencieux, à condition de respecter les instructions reçues, se montre capable d'effectuer un tirage, alors qu'avec Ennadre le temps intervient en force entre les différentes opérations, et surtout pendant l'agrandissement. Cette temporalité s'apparente plus à celle des arts plastiques qu'au temps instantané des photographes.

Mais revenons au négatif retenu : il se présente comme la puissance d'une œuvre non encore passée à l'acte ; il lui manque en effet la lumière. Sorte d'image virtuelle, l'œil et la main de l'artiste accoucheront l'image. Ici, la manière d'Ennadre est fille de celle des peintres de la

Moment«, bei dem er, mit dem Objektiv »ganz nah herangehend«, schließlich den Auslöser betätigt. »Aus nächster Nähe mit einem Auge gesehen, ergeben die plastischen Objekte ein vollkommenes Bild«, schrieb Leonardo da Vinci. Bei einem Photoapparat muß man noch »das Objektiv im Kopf« haben, »sein eigener Entfernungsmesser« sein und über eine intuitive Kenntnis der Einstellung verfügen, Frucht jahrelanger Versuche und Arbeit. Eine so eigenwillige Position legt nahe, daß Ennadre sich eine ganz eigene photographische Wahrnehmung angeeignet hat, bei der er ein Objektiv konstanter Brennweite benutzt: Er arbeitet ausschließlich mit Weitwinkel und verwendet diese objektiv aus allernächster Nähe, nicht etwa um das Gesichtsfeld zu erweitern, sondern um »nahe heranzukommen« – was Puristen erschauern läßt. Indem er im umgekehrten Sinn und widernatürlich diese Brennweite verwendet, die eigentlich der Architektur vorbehalten ist, gibt Ennadre seinem Bild Gestalt und verflacht merklich Tiefenwirkung und Perspektive in diesem Stadium seiner Arbeit. Das ist nur möglich, weil die so behandelte Photographie erst mit der Vergrößerung ihre Endfassung erreicht, für die, wie wir sehen werden, Ennadre ihr Relief verleiht, indem er Licht aufsetzt. Die große Brennweite führt zu einer leichten Verzerrung, die, wenn sie bewußt eingesetzt wird, dazu beiträgt, das Negativbild zu gestalten. Man kann sich kaum vorstellen, wie eine solche Beschreibung der Aufnahmetechnik dazu führen sollte, verbindliche Maße und Einstellungen aufzustellen: Das Leben geht zu schnell vorbei, als daß man seine Zeit damit vergeuden dürfte, Objektive auszuwechseln und an ihren Ringen zu drehen. Daraus ergibt sich, daß der Apparat um der Schärfe willen unverändert auf kürzeste Belichtungszeit und eine mittlere Blende eingestellt bleibt.

Nun ließe sich dagegen fragen, wie kann man dann bei unterschiedlichsten Lichtverhältnissen über genügend Helligkeit verfügen? Ennadre antwortet, indem er seinen Apparat oben und unten mit zwei Blitzlichten versieht, deren Lichtkegel sich im Mittelpunkt des Motivs schneiden. Bei Tag wie bei Nacht kann er mit seinem Licht arbeiten, das immer gleich bleibt und — der Stellung des Objektivs zwangsläufig folgend – ihm erlaubt, Schatten zu beseitigen, denn das Lot fällt senkrecht auf das Motiv, oder sie zu nutzen, indem er sie absichtlich betont, wobei er dann spielerisch mit dem Apparat, d.h. mit der Stellung der Linse im Raum umgeht.

Ennadre richtet sich bei der Entwicklung seiner Negative nach den Gegebenheiten zum Zeitpunkt ihrer Aufnahme. Seine Filme und die Kontaktabzüge sind im Format (6 x 6 cm) zu klein für seine weitere Arbeit. Deshalb macht er Serien von Arbeitsabzügen (24 x 30 cm), um sie prüfen, auswerten und auswählen zu können. Es handelt sich nicht um fertige Werke, sondern um einfache, noch ›flache‹ Papierabzüge, ohne Relief und angemessene Belichtung, noch ganz ohne perspektivische Wirkung. Es sind erst Entwürfe, Skizzen, Formen eines rudimentären Werks, das noch auf die Geburt seines Lichts wartet. Nach kritischer Prüfung werden die meisten Abzüge verworfen: eine unerbittliche Auswahl. Nun stellt Ennadre manchmal zwei- oder dreiteilige Bildfolgen her und beginnt mit der Arbeit an diesen ausgewählten Exemplaren. Auch hier

to black out anything that is not strictly essential. "I'm a painter in the dark", says Ennadre, whose palette is rich with the blacks he uses to define the subject and structure the image with lines and surfaces. Black is the "other", the place occupied by the other, your place and mine: it allows our vision to get its bearings, to appreciate variations in density between different shades of gray and white. There is nothing funereal about it. It acts like a form of lighting that provides relief and contour, the desired depth, thanks to a skilful counterpoint of light and dark that is reminiscent at times of Caravaggio in painting and Murnau or Dreyer in cinema. The composition, meanwhile, establishes tonal harmony: it determines the exact dose of white – "that extreme flash of light" (Alberti) – along with the black and different grays that will be projected, stroke by stroke, onto surfaces defined by a subtle play of masks, and thus the quantity of light. It is at this point that the hesitant waltz of masks begins, each having its own specific duration of light, its own position, form and movement, as it is superimposed and moved about on the paper and in space. This deliberate conjuring trick lasts for hours, for days on end, and results in a large-format print (130 x 160 cm) or "viewing copy", analysis of which will enable Ennadre to correct any final imperfections (only visible in this format) before moving on to the next prints.

But let us return to the house where Ennadre was born, where light, remember, came from on high to illuminate the darkness; for it is here that he today has his laboratory, his cave of making. In it he acts like a designer, composer and sculptor of light, inventing new practices that will allow him to pin down in his images intensities of light that have become exposure times. Darken here, blacken or clarify there, whiten, shade, design masks, lines and surfaces, arrange transitions, and so forth. These different operations make each print unique; the rest, though bearing a family resemblance to their model, will retain their difference and their own identity. The photographs one sees here and there in small formats are merely reproductions, like those made of paintings.

In trying to give a picture of Ennadre's technique, we have limited ourself to areas that help clarify his manner, style and poetics. When speaking of his work, he calls it his "job", experiencing it as a physical and spiritual activity, the only one he has ever really kept to in his life. Neither pleasure nor recreation, his job, without ever losing the unity of the initial project, nevertheless has periods.

Series? Subjects? Themes would be more appropriate – not in a scholarly sense, but in a more metaphysical, timeless and mythical sense, as when Picasso confided to Malraux that he "didn't believe in subjects, but did believe in themes – providing you express them through emblems. . . ." What he called themes were "birth, pregnancy, suffering, murder, couples, death, rebellion, perhaps kissing. . . . They are much older than civilization."

Renaissance qui cherchaient à déterminer le contour de leur figure, sa «circonspection», sa «composition» et enfin la «réception des lumières», selon la terminologie d'Alberti dans son *De Pictura* (1435). Le premier acte revient à dessiner le contour de la figure au centre de l'image à l'aide d'un masque destiné à faire disparaître l'accessoire dans le noir. «Je suis un peintre dans le noir», dit Ennadre dont la palette est riche de noirs qu'il utilise pour délimiter les sujets et structurer l'image avec des lignes et des surfaces. Le noir, c'est «l'autre», la place de l'autre, la vôtre, la mienne: il permet à notre vision de se repérer, d'apprécier la diversité des variations de densité entre les valeurs grises et blanches. Il n'a rien de funèbre, mais se comporte comme un éclairage qui donne le relief et le modelé, la profondeur désirée, grâce à un savant contrepoint entre le clair et l'obscur, entre les lumières et les ombres, rappellant, par moments, des œuvres comme celle de Caravage, en peinture, de Murnau ou de Dreyer, au cinéma. La composition, quant à elle, établit l'harmonie entre les valeurs: elle dose le blanc,«éclat extrême de la lumière» (Alberti), la gamme des gris et le noir qui seront projetés sur les surfaces délimitées par un jeu subtil de caches, touche par touche, et donc la quantité de lumière. Commence alors la valse-hésitation des masques qui se superposent, évoluent, sur le papier et dans l'espace, chacun disposant d'un temps de lumière propre, d'une place, d'une forme et d'un mouvement. Cette séance de magie calculée occupe de longues heures, des journées entières, et aboutit à un tirage grand format (130 x 160 cm), l'exemplaire de vision, dont l'analyse permettra d'établir les suivants, compte tenu de la correction des dernières imperfections, perceptibles seulement à ce format.

Mais revenons à la maison natale d'Ennadre: ce lieu où, souvenons-nous, la lumière venait d'en haut illuminer le noir, c'est aujourd'hui son laboratoire, l'antre de son alchimie. Il s'y comporte en dessinateur, compositeur et sculpteur de lumière, inventant des pratiques nouvelles pour fixer dans ses images les intensités lumineuses devenues temps d'exposition. Foncer ici, noircir, éclairer là, blanchir, ombrer, dessiner les masques, les lignes et les surfaces, aménager les transitions... Autant d'opérations qui font de chaque tirage une œuvre unique ; les autre auront un air de famille avec leur modèle, mais garderont leur différence et leur identité propre. Les photographies que l'on peut voir en petit format, ici ou là, ne sont que de simples reproductions, comme on en fait pour les tableaux.

Notre évocation de la technique d' Ennadre s'est limitée à ce qui éclaire sa manière, son style et sa poétique. Lorsqu'il parle de son œuvre, il l'appelle son «travail», la vivant comme une activité physique et spirituelle, la seule à laquelle il se soit vraiment tenu dans sa vie. Ni loisir, ni divertissement, ce travail, sans jamais perdre l'unité du projet initial, a cependant ses périodes. Séries, sujets ? Thèmes conviendrait mieux, non pas dans le sens scolaire, mais définis dans un registre métaphysique, intemporel et mythique,

setzt er sich von der traditionellen Photographie ab, bei der ein gewissenhafter Laborant, wenn er die vorgegebenen Instruktionen beachtet, Abzüge herstellen kann. Bei Ennadre hingegen hat zwischen den verschiedenen Arbeitsgängen, und vor allem während der Vergrößerung, die Zeit entscheidenden Einfluß. Dieser Zeitfaktor gehört eher in den Bereich der bildenden Kunst als zu dem Begriff des kurzen Moments in der Photographie.

Kommen wir jedoch zum ausgewählten Negativ zurück: Es erscheint wie das Schöpferische im Werk, das seine Gestalt noch nicht gefunden hat – es fehlt ihm noch das Licht. Es ist eine Art virtuelles Bild, aus dem Auge und Hand des Künstlers erst das eigentliche Bild hervorbringen. Hier ist Ennadre in seiner Arbeitsweise den Malern der Renaissance nahe, deren Anliegen die Kontur ihrer Gestalten war, ihr ›Umriß‹, ihre ›Komposition‹ und schließlich der ›Lichteinfall‹, gemäß der Terminologie Albertis in seiner Schrift *De Pictura* (1435). Die erste Handlung besteht darin, mit Hilfe einer Maske, die alles übrige in Schwarz verschwinden läßt, die Kontur der Gestalt im Zentrum des Bildes nachzuziehen. »Ich bin ein Maler in Schwarz«, sagt Ennadre, dessen Palette reich an Schwarztönen ist, die er verwendet, um die Motive abzugrenzen und das Bild mit Hilfe von Linien und Abstufungen zu strukturieren. Das Schwarze, das ist das ›Andere‹, die Stelle des anderen, Ihre, meine: Es erlaubt unserer Sicht, sich zurechtzufinden, die Verschiedenartigkeit der Abstufungen zwischen den Grau- und Weißtönen einzuschätzen. Es hat nichts Düsteres, verhält sich eher wie eine Beleuchtung, die Relief, Form und erwünschte Tiefe erzeugt, dank eines gekonnten Kontrapunkts zwischen Helligkeit und Dunkel, zwischen Licht und Schatten. Teilweise erinnert dies in der Malerei an Werke eines Caravaggio, im Film an Murnau oder Dreyer. Erst die Komposition bringt die Einzelwerte zu einer Harmonie: Sie dosiert das Weiß, den »stärksten Lichteffekt« (Alberti), die verschiedenen Grautöne und das Schwarz. Sie werden mit der entsprechenden Lichtmenge, abgegrenzt durch ein überaus feinsinniges Abdeckungsspiel, auf die Bildoberfläche projiziert. Damit beginnt der Wechseltanz der Masken, die sich übereinander legen, sich auf dem Papier und im Raum entwickeln, jede mit ihrer eigenen Lichtzeit, ihrem eigenen Platz, ihrer Form und ihrer Bewegung. Diese Sitzung ausgeklügelter Magie nimmt Stunde um Stunde ganze Tage in Anspruch und führt zu dem Exemplar visionärer Schau, einem großformatigen Abzug (130 x 160 cm), der nach Analyse und unter sorgfältiger Beseitigung der letzten Mängel, die nur in diesem Format sichtbar werden, die Herstellung eines endgültigen Abzuges erlaubt.

Kommen wir zum Geburtshaus Ennadres zurück, zu jenem Ort, an dem das Licht von oben das Schwarz erhellte: Heute ist es das Licht in seinem Laboratorium, seiner Alchimistenhöhle. Er arbeitet darin als Zeichner, Komponist und Bildhauer des Lichts, erfindet neue Verfahren, mit denen er Lichtintensitäten auf seinen Bildern festhält, die zu Belichtungszeiten geworden sind. Hier das Dunkle verstärken, schwärzen, dort lichter machen, Weiß zusetzen, Schatten auflegen, Masken, Linien, Oberflächen zeichnen, Übergänge einrichten ... so viele Arbeitsgänge, die aus jedem Abzug ein Unikat

In chronological order, Ennadre's themes are as follows:

1976 His mother's funeral, cemetery, first *Hands* (Casablanca – death)
1978-82 *Hands, back, feet* (Asia – the body)
1982-83 *Birth* (the Hôtel-Dieu in Paris)
1985 *Slaughterhouse* (In Stockholm, Munich and Marrakech – violence and death)
1985-90 *Herculaneum* (Memory and death)
1987 *Print of the Hanged Man* (Paris area – suicide or murder)
1989 *Gravestones and Paving-Stones from the Medina in Fez*
1990 *Lascaux* (the birth of art)
1991 *Paleontological Traces* (Karlsruhe, Messel – the origin)
1991 *Notre-Dame de Paris*
1992 *Auschwitz*
1992 *The Man in the Ice* (South Tyrol, Austria)
1992-93 *Squid and Fish* (Al Madrhabath in Arabic, the Straits of Gibraltar – violence and death)
1993-95 *Trance* (Benin, Haiti)
1995 *L'Alhambra* (Spain)
1996 *Ay! mi Toro!* (Arles, France)

The reader will already have sensed that Ennadre, when he remarks that every subject he touches "relates to death", is giving us a close-up of the centre of gravity of his work. Death, the heart of his concern, does not mean abolition, emptiness, the end or void; it no more inhabits the crepuscular, the morbid, the macabre or the infernal than it appeals to the Beyond. The religious-minded, whatever their Koran, leave him cold: he thinks of them as conjurers who try to conceal the poverty of their lives, dangerous purveyors of violence and fanaticism. There is no place for the infinite in images which, "taken at very close range", plunge distant perspectives into darkness; nor for the uncanny, because the space with which Ennadre is concerned is that of the tragic. The death at work in his photographs is defined by life, "a set of functions that resist death" according to the physician Bichat, what Ennadre would call "death-life". All that matters is the accord, problematic and tragic, between these two facets of a reality that there can be no question of reproducing, only of "forming", figuring and experiencing. Not death as severance, but death as structuring life, a structured life, "giving birth to life". A life that enjoys a soothing sense of affinity with death, a sense of complicity like that evoked by Mozart in a letter to his father: "As death, when we come to consider it closely, is the true goal of our existence, I have formed over the last few years such close relations with this best and truest friend of mankind that his image is not only no longer terrifying to me, but is indeed very soothing and

comme lorsque Picasso confiait à Malraux qu'il «ne croyait pas aux sujets, mais croyait aux thèmes – à condition de les exprimer par des emblèmes...» Il appelait thèmes «la naissance, la grossesse, la souffrance, le meurtre, le couple, la mort, la révolte, peut-être le baiser... Ils viennent de plus loin que la civilisation.»

Chronologiquement, les thèmes d'Ennadre sont les suivants:

1976 Enterrement de sa mère, cimetière, premières *Mains* (Casablanca – la mort)
1978-82 *Les Mains, le dos, les pieds* (Asie – le corps)
1982-83 *Accouchements* (Hôtel-Dieu à Paris – la naissance)
1985 *Boucherie* (Abattoirs de Stockholm, Munich, Marrakech – la violence et la mort)
1985-90 *Les Morts exhumés d'Herculaneum* (la mémoire, la mort)
1987 *L'Empreinte du pendu* (Région parisienne – le suicide ou le meurtre)
1989 *Pierres tombales et pavés de la Médina de Fès*
1990 *Les fresques de Lascaux* (la naissance de l'art)
1991 *Vestiges paléontologiques* (Karlsruhe, Messel – l'origine)
1991 *Notre-Dame de Paris*
1992 *Auschwitz*
1992 *L'Homme des glaces* (Tyrol du Sud).
1992-93 *Pêches et poulpes* (madragues, Al Madrhabath en arabe, Détroit de Gibraltar – la violence et la mort)
1993-95 *Transes* (Le Bénin, Haïti)
1995 *L'Alhambra* (Espagne)
1996 *Ay! mi toro!* (Arles)

Notre lecteur a déjà senti qu'Ennadre, lorsqu'il précise que tous les sujets auxquels il touche «ont rapport avec la mort», fait un gros plan sur le centre de gravité de son œuvre. La mort, au vif de son intérêt, n'est pas abolition, vide, fin ou néant; elle n'évolue pas dans le crépusculaire, le morbide, le macabre ou l'infernal, pas plus qu'elle n'en appelle à un quelconque Au-delà. Les religieux, quel que soit leur Coran, le laissent froid: il ne voit en eux qu'illusionnistes jouant à cache-misère et dangereux pourvoyeurs de violence et de fanatisme. Aucune place pour l'infini dans ses images qui, «s'approchant au plus près», plongent dans le noir les perspectives lointaines, ni pour le fantastique, parce que son espace est celui du tragique. La mort qui œuvre dans son travail se définit par la vie, «ensemble des fonctions qui résistent à la mort», d'après le médecin Bichat, la «mort-vie», dirait Ennadre. Seul compte l'accord, problématique et tragique, entre ces deux aspects d'une même réalité qu'il ne saurait être question de reproduire, mais de «former» de figurer et de vivre. Non pas mort-

machen. Weitere sehen zwar dem Modell ähnlich, bleiben jedoch unterschieden von ihm und behalten somit ihre Eigenheit. Photographien, die man im Kleinformat hie und da zu sehen bekommt, sind nur einfache Reproduktionen, wie man sie von Gemälden herstellt.

Bei der Vorstellung von Ennadres Technik haben wir uns darauf beschränkt, seine Arbeitsweise, seinen Stil und seine schöpferische Fähigkeit zu beleuchten. Wenn er von seinem Werk spricht, nennt er es seine ›Arbeit‹, die er wie eine physische und geistige Arbeit erlebt, bei der er als der einzigen in seinem Leben wirklich geblieben ist. Keine Freizeit, keine Zerstreuungen, und doch hat diese Arbeit Schwerpunktzeiten, ohne je das einheitliche Ausgangskonzept zu verlassen. Serien, Motive? Besser paßt das Wort ›Themen‹, nicht im schulischen Sinn, sondern von einer metaphysischen Kategorie bestimmt, zeitlos, sinnbildhaft, wie bei Picasso, der zu Malraux sagte, daß er »nicht an Motive, sondern an Themen glaubt – vorausgesetzt, daß sie in Sinnbildern ausgedrückt werden ...«. Als Themen nannte dieser »Geburt, Schwangerschaft, Leid, Mord, das Paar, Tod, Revolte, vielleicht den Kuß ... Ihr Ursprung liegt lange vor der Zivilisation«.

Chronologisch sind Ennadres Themen die folgenden:

1976 Beisetzung der Mutter, Friedhof, erste *Hände* (Casablanca – der Tod)
1978-82 *Hände, Rücken, Füße* (Asien – der Körper)
1982-83 *Geburt* (Hôtel-Dieu in Paris)
1985 *Schlachthof* (Schlachthöfe von Stockholm, München, Marrakesch – Gewalt und Tod)
1985-90 *Die Exhumierten von Herculaneum* (Erinnerung, Tod)
1987 *Der Abdruck des Erhängten* (Region Paris – Selbstmord oder Mord)
1989 *Grabsteine und Pflastersteine der Medina von Fès*
1990 Die Wandbilder von *Lascaux* (Ursprung der Kunst)
1991 *Paläontologische Spuren* (Karlsruhe, Messel – der Ursprung)
1991 *Notre-Dame de Paris*
1992 *Auschwitz*
1992 *Der Mensch aus dem Eis* (Südtirol)
1992-93 *Tintenfisch und Fische* (Thunfischnetze, Al Madrhabath auf Arabisch; Straße von Gibraltar – Gewalt und Tod)
1993-95 *Trance* (Bénin, Haiti)
1995 *L'Alhambra* (Spanien)
1996 *Ay! mi toro!* (Arles)

Es wurde bereits deutlich, daß Ennadre, wenn er erklärt, alle Motive, an die er herangeht, hätten »mit dem Tod zu tun«, in Großaufnahme auf den Schwerpunkt seines Werkes verweist. Der Tod, dem sein lebhaftestes Interesse gilt, hat nichts Zerstörerisches, ist nicht leer, nicht endlich oder gar ein

consoling!" In observing that "the West rejects birth and death", Ennadre overlaps with a thought of Barthes' in *La Chambre claire. Notes sur la photographie*: "For Death, in a society, has to be somewhere; if it is no longer (or less so) in the religious, it must be elsewhere: perhaps in this image that produces Death by wanting to preserve life. Contemporary with the retreat of rites, Photography might be said to correspond to the intrusion, in our modern society, of a Death that is asymbolic, outside religion, outside ritual, a sort of abrupt plunge into literal Death. Life/Death: the paradigm is reduced to a mere trigger mechanism separating the initial pose from the final paper." Even at the time of his mother's funeral, Ennadre's first photographs had nothing gloomy about them: no tears, no coffin, only the resistance of pain in the skin and bones of hands tense with suffering. An affirmation of life in the immanence of its tragic condition. This crucial experience of death would be extended far into space and time: such was the long voyage in Asia and *Hands, back, feet.* Ennadre's original intention was to "do a work about the body" – the body immersed in life, and on no account the body posing. Where might suitable settings be found for a project of this kind? Asia, its streets and trains teeming with people, seemed to live up to his expectations, especially since the sheer remoteness and material difficulties of the undertaking gave him a sense of distance that helped provide the concentration he needed. It was a question, not of representing suffering like a reporter or indulging in a complacent display of human misery, but of drawing out the figure of suffering itself, the suffering he felt in others and in himself. He made ready, then, for the "true encounters" that would allow him to "figure" the body of that suffering in his pyramid of light. Hands that reach out or intertwine, their lines leaving an impress on time as furrows do on earth. Illuminated fingerprints. Bones and wrinkled skin, in the quick of suffering. Hands snatched from darkness: an enchanted light. Anyone who looks at these hands with eyes as searching as those they turn on us, allowing his attention to focus on the dots – small spaces and lines, white, gray or black – formed by the play of lights, will see that the perspective in question is anything but realistic. Each stroke of light is a sheer product of the artist's will, a reflection. The logic is not one of reproduction or representation, not one of expression even, but of imagination. Where else has one seen the abrupt slope of a spinal column like that in *Back of Light*, folded like an eroded mountain and violently lit up by a snuffed torch held by an arm with tortured veins that plunges the nearby head into a darkness that, to say the least, is enigmatic? Where, then, is the photo? It has ceased to exist. We are almost faced with an etching, a mezzotint engraving, a Chinese-ink drawing, a painting, I don't know what.

The body bursting into life: in *Deliveries at Hôtel-Dieu*, Ennadre came face to face with birth. Flesh in tension, forceps and skulls taking life by force. A child who has just emerged from its mother's womb, its eyes and fists closed, its mouth open, screams at the world after its first hand-to-hand combat. Another, marked by the darkness of first

coupure, mais mort structurante de la vie, vie structurée, « donnant vie à la vie ». Vivre avec la mort un rapport d'affinité apaisante, de complicité, comparable à celui qu'évoquait Mozart, écrivant à son père : « Comme la mort (à y regarder de plus près) est le vrai but de la vie, je me suis, depuis quelques années, tellement familiarisé avec cette véritable et parfaite amie de l'homme que son image non seulement n'a plus rien d'effrayant pour moi, mais m'est très apaisante, très consolante. » Constatant que « l'Occident refuse la naissance et la mort », Ennadre croise la pensée du Barthes de *La Chambre claire. Notes sur la photographie* : « car la Mort, dans une société, il faut bien qu'elle soit quelque part ; si elle n'est plus (ou est moins) dans le religieux, elle doit être ailleurs : peut-être dans cette image qui produit la Mort en voulant conserver la vie. Contemporaine du recul des rites, la Photographie correspondrait peut-être à l'intrusion, dans notre société moderne, d'une Mort asymbolique, hors religion, hors rituel, sorte de plongée brusque dans la Mort littérale. La Vie / la Mort : le paradigme se réduit à un simple déclic, celui qui sépare la pose initiale du papier final. »

Déjà lors de l'enterrement de sa mère, les premières photographies d'Ennadre n'avaient rien de funèbre : ni larmes, ni cercueil, mais résistance de la douleur dans les os et la peau des mains crispées par la souffrance. Affirmation de la vie dans l'immanence de sa condition tragique. Cette expérience cruciale de la mort devait se prolonger loin, loin dans l'espace et dans le temps : ce fut alors le long voyage en Asie et *Les Mains, le dos, les pieds*. L'intention première était de « faire un travail sur le corps », le corps immergé dans la vie, et surtout pas le corps en train de poser. Où rencontrer des situations adéquates au projet ? L'Asie, sa marée humaine dans les rues et les trains lui semblèrent à la hauteur de son attente, d'autant plus que le grand éloignement et les difficultés matérielles de l'entreprise lui procuraient l'effet de distanciation propice à l'effort de concentration nécessaire. Pas question de représenter la souffrance à la manière d'un reporter, ni de se livrer à l'étalage complaisant de la misère humaine, mais extraire la figure de la souffrance elle-même, celle qu'il ressent chez les autres et en lui-même. Il se mit donc en demeure d'être prêt pour les « rencontres vraies » qu'il espérait, afin de « figurer » le corps de cette souffrance dans sa pyramide de lumière. Mains entrelacées, mains tendues, dont les lignes impriment le temps, comme le sillon la terre. Empreintes digitales enluminées. Os et peaux parcheminées, au vif de la souffrance. Mains arrachées aux ténèbres : luminescence magique. Qui fixe ces mains avec des yeux aussi pénétrants que ceux avec lesquels elles vous regardent et se laisse capter par les points, petits espaces et traits, blancs, gris ou noirs, du jeu des valeurs de la lumière verra que l'on est bel et bien en dehors de toute perspective réaliste. Chaque touche de lumière est pure volonté d'artiste, réflexion. La logique n'est pas celle de la reproduction, de la représentation ni même de l'expression, mais celle de l'imaginaire. A-t-on vu ailleurs que dans

Nichts; der Tod entwickelt sich nicht aus Zwielichtigem, Krankhaftem, Makabrem oder aus Vorstellungen der Hölle, ebensowenig wie er sich auf ein irgendwie geartetes Jenseits bezieht. Ennadre lassen die Gläubigen kalt, ganz gleich, wie ihr Koran auch heißen mag. Er sieht in ihnen nur Illusionisten, die mit dem Elend Versteck spielen und gefährliche Gewalt- und Fanatismusstifter sind. Kein Platz für das Unendliche in seinen Bildern, die, »da sie ganz nahe dran sind«, Perspektiven der Ferne ins Schwarze tauchen; auch kein Platz fürs Phantastische, denn sein Raum ist der des Tragischen. Der Tod, der in seinem Werk wirkt, ist durch das Leben definiert, nach Worten des Arztes Bichat »das Gesamt der Funktionen, die dem Tod widerstehen«. Ennadre würde sagen das »Todleben«. Was zählt, ist allein die problematische, tragische Eintracht zwischen den beiden Aspekten ein und derselben Wirklichkeit, die es nicht etwa zu reproduzieren, sondern nur zu ›formen‹, sich vorzustellen und zu leben gilt. Kein Tod, der das Leben abbricht, sondern einer, der aufbaut, gegliedertes Leben ist, der ›dem Leben Lebendigkeit gibt‹. Mit dem Tod in beruhigender, vertrauter Beziehung leben, etwa wie Mozart, der an seinen Vater schreibt: »Da der Tod, (wenn man näher hinschaut), das wahre Ziel des Lebens ist, habe ich mich seit einigen Jahren mit diesem echten und vollkommenen Freund des Menschen so vertraut gemacht, daß sein Bild bei mir nicht nur keinen Schrecken hervorruft, sondern beruhigend und sehr tröstlich auf mich wirkt.« Mit der Feststellung, daß »westliche Einstellung Geburt und Tod zurückweist«, begegnet Ennadre dem Denken eines Roland Barthes in *Die helle Kammer. Bemerkungen zur Photographie*: »Denn in einer Gesellschaft muß der Tod irgendwo doch sein. Wenn er nicht mehr (oder eher weniger) im Religiösen ist, muß er anderswo sein, vielleicht in jenem Bild, das, indem es das Leben bewahren will, den TOD hervorbringt. Die Photographie könnte der rückläufigen Praxis im Religiösen, dem Einzug eines nicht mehr sinnbildlichen Todes in unserer modernen Gesellschaft, entsprechen, außerhalb von Religion, außerhalb der Riten, eine Art abruptes Eindringen in den buchstäblichen Tod. Das Leben/ der Tod: Das Paradigma beschränkt sich auf ein einfaches Klick, das die Ausgangseinstellung vom fertigen Papier trennt.«

Schon bei der Beerdigung seiner Mutter hatten Ennadres erste Photographien nichts Trauriges: Weder Tränen noch Sarg, sondern Widerstand des Schmerzes in Knochen und Haut der Hände, verkrampft vom Schmerz, eine Bejahung des Lebens in seiner irdischen, tragischen Bedingtheit. Diese entscheidende Erfahrung des Todes sollte sich lange, sehr lange in Zeit und Raum fortsetzen: Sie wurde zu der langen Reise nach Asien und zur Serie der *Hände, Rücken, Füße*. Zunächst bestand die Absicht, »eine Arbeit über den Körper zu machen«, den Körper mitten im Leben zu zeigen, nicht etwa in Pose. Wo waren entsprechende Situationen für ein solches Projekt zu finden? Asien mit seiner Menschenflut in Straßen und Eisenbahnen schien seiner Erwartung in hohem Maß zu entsprechen, umso mehr, als die große Entfernung und die materiellen Schwierigkeiten des Unterfangens ihm die Distanz verschaffen konnten, die einer notwendigen Bemühung um Konzentration günstig ist. Es ging ihm nicht darum, Leid in der Art einer Reportage

things, its forms still distended, frolics about in a shimmering chiaroscuro of blood. And because "birth is already death", there is the shattering magic beauty of this little form, already no longer wholly human, couched in eternal sleep, shrouded in the darkness that defines the outline of its body, folded with light, mummified almost, petrified in silence, like a destiny: *Moira.* Attention should also be paid to those balls of light, those scintillating stars that Ennadre has created for us, discovering them in placentas irrigated by a network of vessels and seething with life like the world itself.

15 In a different vein, Ennadre has tackled blood and the body, the bruised, slaughtered and dismembered bodies of beasts in the violence of slaughterhouses (*Slaughterhouse,* 1985): "It's incredible, as though the beasts know they're going to die. They screamed and were electrocuted. Their killers were drinking cans of beer. For them, it was a game. It was madness. Consider the displacement: the beasts were the men, and the humans, the beasts". Meat, the incarnation of violence and death, bursts forth in these images, these carved-up bodies "without organs", as Artaud wrote: "The body is the body It stands alone It has no need of organs The body is never an organism Organisms are the enemies of bodies".

Gilles Deleuze, in *Francis Bacon: The Logic of Sensation,* comments: "The body without organs is an intense body, an intensive body. The Figure is precisely the body without organs. Meat is that state of the body in which flesh and bones merge locally. Meat is not dead flesh, it retains all its sufferings. Bacon does not say 'Pity the beasts', but rather that every man who suffers is meat. Meat is the zone common to both man and beast. The painter is a butcher". Deleuze then cites Bacon himself: "I've always been very moved by pictures about slaughterhouses and meat, and to me they belong very much to the whole thing of the Crucifixion. Well, of course, we are meat, we are potential carcasses. If I go into a butcher's shop I always think it's surprising that I wasn't there instead of the animal". Deleuze comments: "The man who suffers is a beast, the beast that suffers is a man. That is the reality of becoming. What revolutionary figure in art, politics, religion, or in anything you like, has not felt that extreme moment when he was no more than a beast, and become, not answerable for the calves who die, but answerable to the calves who die?" This philosophic reading of the work of one of our century's great painters is very close to what we experience with Ennadre's *Slaughterhouse;* Ennadre, moreover, has produced his self-portrait by projecting the imaginary outline of his face onto a background of meat. It would be stupid to raise the question of resemblance, since it is obvious that, under such circumstances, "the head-meat is the animal-future of man" as it is for Deleuze.

Ennadre's manner is never illustrative, narrative or figurative, but "figural"; "free the Figure", "rescue the Figure from the figurative", these Deleuzian expressions adequately characterize the sense of his approach. Though his images sometimes border

Le Dos de lumière une telle descente de colonne vertébrale, plissée comme une montagne érodée, violemment éclairée par une torche éteinte que tient un bras aux veines torturées et qui plonge la tête toute proche dans un noir pour le moins énigmatique ? Mais où est donc la photo ? Il n'y en a plus. Nous sommes presque devant une eau-forte, une gravure à la manière noire, un dessin à l'encre de Chine, un tableau, que sais-je ?

Irruption du corps dans la vie : lors des *Accouchements à l'Hôtel-Dieu,* Ennadre se confronta à la naissance. Chairs en tension, fers et crânes forçant la vie. Cet enfant, juste sorti du ventre de sa mère, yeux et poings fermés, bouche ouverte, cri sur le monde après son premier combat au corps à corps. Cet autre, marqué du noir originaire, aux formes encore distendues, qui s'ébat dans le miroitement clair-obscur du sang. Et, parce que « la naissance, c'est déjà la mort », la sidérante beauté magique de cette petite forme, déjà plus totalement humaine, couchée dans l'éternel sommeil, ensevelie dans le noir qui dessine le contour de son corps plissé de lumière, presque momifié, pétrifié dans le silence, comme un destin : Moïra. On s'arrêtera aussi surces boules de lumière, astres scintillants, qu'Ennadre créa pour nous, les découvrant dans les placentas irrigués par un enchevêtrement de vaisseaux, vivants comme le bouillonnement du monde.

Ennadre, dans un autre registre, s'est affronté au sang et à la chair, aux corps meurtris, tués et dépecés des bêtes dans la violence des abattoirs, ce sera *Boucherie* (1985) : « C'est fou, comme les bêtes savent qu'elles vont mourir. Elles gueulaient, on les électrocutait. Et les tueurs buvaient des canettes de bière : pour eux, c'était un jeu. C'était la folie. Voyez ce déplacement : les bêtes, c'étaient les hommes, et les humains, les bêtes. » Les viandes, incarnation de la violence et de la mort, éclatent dans les images, corps morcelés « , sans organe », comme l'écrivait Artaud : « Le corps est le corps Il est seul Et n'a pas besoin d'organe Le corps n'est jamais un organisme Les organismes sont les ennemis du corps. »

Gilles Deleuze, dans *Francis Bacon, Logique de la sensation,* commente : « Le corps sans organe ... c'est un corps intense, intensif ... La Figure, c'est précisément le corps sans organe ... La viande est cet état du corps où la chair et les os se confondent localement ... La viande n'est pas une chair morte, elle a gardé toutes les souffrances ... Bacon ne dit pas "pitié pour les bêtes", mais plutôt tout homme qui souffre est de la viande. La viande est la zone commune de l'homme et de la bête ... Le peintre est boucher ... » Deleuze cite alors Bacon lui-même : « J'ai toujours été touché par les images relatives aux abattoirs et à la viande, et pour moi elles sont liées étroitement à tout ce qu'est la Crucifixion ... C'est sûr, nous sommes de la viande, nous sommes des carcasses en puissance. Si je vais chez un boucher, je trouve toujours surprenant de ne pas être là, à la place de l'animal. » Deleuze précise : « L'homme qui souffre est une bête, la bête qui souffre est un homme. C'est la réalité du devenir. Quel homme révolutionnaire en art, en politique,

wiederzugeben, auch nicht, sich der gefälligen Ausstellung menschlichen Elends zu widmen. Ennadre will vielmehr die Gestalt des Leids herausfiltern, wie er sie bei den anderen und bei sich selbst empfindet. So traf er seine Vorbereitung auf die ›echten Begegnungen‹, die er erhoffte, um das Korpus dieses Leids in seiner Lichtpyramide zu ›gestalten‹. Ineinander verschlungene Hände, ausgestreckte Hände, in deren Linien die Zeit wie die Furche in der Erde eingekerbt ist. Ausgeleuchtete Fingerabdrücke. Schmerzerfüllte pergamentene Knochen und Häute. Hände, die der Finsternis entrissen sind: ein magisches Nachleuchten. Wer diese Hände ebenso durchdringend anschaut, wie sie einen fixieren, und sich von den Punkten, den kleinen Zwischenräumen und Zeichnungen in Weiß, Grau oder Schwarz, vom Spiel der Lichtwerte packen läßt, bemerkt sicher, daß man wirklich jeder realistischen Perspektive entrückt ist. Jeder Lichttupfer ist reiner Willensausdruck des Künstlers, ist überlegt. Das Zwingende liegt nicht in der Wiedergabe, auch nicht in der Darstellung oder gar im Ausdruck, es liegt im Imaginären. Hat man je sonst wie im Bild des *Rückens* einen solchen Wirbelsäulenverlauf gesehen, der wie ein ausgewaschener Berg im grellen Licht einer doch erloschenen Fackel aufgefaltet ist, die ein Arm mit Adern gleich gewundenen Seilen hält und die einen ganz nahen Kopf in ein zumindest rätselhaftes Schwarz taucht? Wo ist denn dann das Photo? Es gibt keines mehr. Wir befinden uns gleichsam vor einer Radierung, einer Tuschzeichnung, vor einem Bild, was weiß man?

Sprung eines Körpers ins Leben: Ennadre beobachtet im Pariser Hôtel-Dieu Geburten. Gespannter Leib, Eisen und Schädel, die das Leben erzwingen. Jenes Kind, das gerade aus dem Bauch seiner Mutter mit geballten Fäusten, geschlossenen Augen und offenem Mund geschlüpft ist, nach seinem ersten Kampf, Leib an Leib, mit dem Schrei über die Welt. Jenes andere, vom Dunkel des Ursprungs gezeichnet, mit noch gelösten Formen, das im gespiegelten Helldunkel des Blutes strampelt. Und weil »die Geburt ja schon der Tod ist«, die verblüffend magische Schönheit dieser kleinen Form, noch nicht ganz Mensch, in ewigen Schlaf gebettet, eingehüllt ins Schwarz. Der Umriß seines vom Licht kraus wirkenden Körpers, fast mumienhaft, in Stille versteinert, vom Schicksal gezeichnet: Moïra. Man wird auch bei den Lichtkugeln, den glänzenden Gestirnen innehalten, die Ennadre für uns so schuf, wie er sie in den von einem Gewirr von Gefäßen durchzogenen Mutterkuchen entdeckt, in denen es lebendig wie im Weltenwirbel zugeht.

Ennadre hat Blut und Fleisch in einem anderen Zusammenhang wahrgenommen: gepeinigte, getötete und in Stücke gerissene Tierkörper in der Gewalt des *Schlachthofs* (1985): »Es ist verrückt, wie die Tiere mitbekommen, daß sie sterben werden. Sie brüllten, und man tötete sie durch Stromstöße. Dabei tranken die Schlächter flaschenweise Bier: Für sie war es nur ein Spiel. Es war irrsinnig. Schauen Sie sich eine derartige Vertauschung an: Die Tiere waren Menschen, die Menschen waren Tiere.« Tierisches Fleisch, Inbegriff von Gewalt und Tod, leuchtet in den Bildern auf, zerstückelte Körper »ohne Organe«, wie Artaud schrieb: »Der Körper ist der Körper. Er steht für sich und braucht keine Organe. Der Körper ist niemals Organismus. Orga-

on abstraction, they are never anchored in it once and for all, for it is the Figure and the sensation produced by violence that he seeks. "What interests me is what lies behind the subject, birth, death, as a way out of violence. Massacres and barbarity, I've seen them in the slaughterhouses. My light tries to mend this horrible violence, showing the horror of this violence, and not the spectacles of horror it produces". His aim is to recover through memory the violence he has experienced, to close in on violence everywhere he sees it in order to distance us from it and exorcise it by "releasing a feeling of nonviolence". And Deleuze concludes: "The violence of sensation stands opposed to the violence of that which is represented (the sensational, the clichéd). The former is inseparable from its direct action on the nervous system, the levels through which it passes, the domains it traverses: itself a Figure, it has nothing of the nature of a figurative object. As in Artaud, cruelty is not what we think, and depends less and less on what is represented".

The series *Herculaneum (1985-90)* has the beauty of a resurrection. Ennadre does not photograph the dead, but the precise moment when the archaeologist at last frees them from the lava of the volcano. In the museum they will soon be reduced to neat rows of bones, washed and classified. But at the moment of their discovery it is a memory that emerges; radiant skeletons recall the fear they once entrusted to the earth; they have not moved since the day of their burial almost two thousand years ago. Their reappearance was unimaginable, as though time had come to a standstill, as though death had finally lost the fight. The abolition of history, the eternal return, the triumph, not of death, but of memory. Defying time in this way projects the work into myth, where, in order to explain the mysteries of the world, fabulous images are invented, as here. The fantastic element in myth transfigures this small body, almost a skeleton, half shadow, half shadow-bearer, as it emerges from its tomb, shaken by the rays of a sepulchral sun; in Ennadre's icons, myth spreads the power of its magic everywhere, becoming a cosmos, a universe.

The more mythogenetic the work, the greater its mythological power, the more Ennadre the individual is hidden, the more his presence is obscured: he would like to disappear completely into his work, to dissolve in it, for at that point it would no longer have need of him but exist as self-evidently universal, freed from its progenitor. In achieving this, he would have rediscovered the true status of the artist: not as an overvalued ego, a star, merely as an absent framework, a useless circumstance, a subject in the original sense of "that which is under", at degree zero, that which gives precedence to the form or Figure, the substance and mythological power of the finally existing work whose autonomy resides in its symbolic function alone. This desire to abolish and bury himself in his work is expressed by Ennadre with unusual acuity in *Print of the Hanged Man* (1987), which he sometimes calls *Self-Portrait II:* "To arrive at zero-being; to be none of my own doing; to eliminate

en religion ou en n'importe quoi, n'a pas senti ce moment extrême où il n'était rien qu'une bête, et devenait responsable non pas des veaux qui meurent, mais devant les veaux qui meurent.» Quelle proximité entre cette lecture philosophique de l'œuvre d'un grand peintre de notre siècle et ce que nous ressentons devant les *Boucheries* d'Ennadre qui a, par ailleurs, cliché son autoportrait, projetant le contour imaginaire de sa figure sur un fond de viandes. Qu'il serait stupide de se poser la question de la ressemblance, tant il est clair qu'en la circonstance, comme pour Deleuze: «La tête-viande, c'est le devenir-animal de l'homme.»

Le mode d'Ennadre n'est jamais illustratif, narratif, ni figuratif, mais «figural», «libérer la Figure», «arracher la Figure au figuratif», autant d'expressions deleuziennes qui caractérisent adéquatement le sens de sa démarche. Si parfois ses images se rapprochent de l'abstraction, elles ne s'y ancrent jamais définitivement car il poursuit la Figure et la sensation émanant de la violence: «Moi, ce qui m'intéresse, c'est ce qu'il y a derrière le sujet, la naissance, la mort, afin de sortir de la violence. Les massacres et la barbarie, je les ai vus dans les abattoirs. Cette violence horrible, ma lumière essaie de la réparer, montrant l'horreur de cette violence, et non pas les spectacles d'horreur qu'elle produit.» Retrouver dans la mémoire la violence vécue, s'en approcher partout où il la voit afin de nous en éloigner et l'exorciser en «déclenchant le sentiment de non-violence». Et Deleuze de conclure: «A la violence du représenté (le sensationnel, le cliché) s'oppose la violence de la sensation. Celle-ci ne fait qu'un avec son action directe sur le système nerveux, les niveaux par lesquels elle passe, les domaines qu'elle traverse: Figure elle-même, elle ne doit rien à la nature d'un objet figuré. C'est comme chez Artaud: la cruauté n'est pas ce que l'on croit, et dépend de moins en moins de ce qui est représenté.»

Les Morts exhumés d' Herculaneum (1985-90) ont la beauté d'une résurrection. Ennadre n'y photographie pas les morts, mais le moment précis où l'archéologue les libère enfin de la lave du volcan. Au musée, ils ne seront bientôt plus qu'alignements d'os rangés, lavés et classés. Mais à l'instant où on les découvre, c'est une mémoire qui surgit ; des squelettes lumineux se rappellent l'effroi qu'ils ont confié à la terre ; ils n'ont pas bougé depuis le jour de leur enfouissement, il y a presque 2000 ans. Leur réapparition était inimaginable, comme si le temps s'était immobilisé, comme si la mort avait finalement perdu la partie. Abolition de l'histoire, éternel retour, triomphe non de la mort, mais de la mémoire. Ce défi au temps projette l'œuvre dans le mythe où s'inventent, pour expliquer les mystères du monde, comme ici justement, des images fabuleuses. Le merveilleux du mythe transfigure ce petit corps presque squelette, mi-ombre mi-ombre portée, qui commence à s'extraire du caveau, ébranlé par les rayons d'un soleil sépulcral ; dans les icônes d'Ennadre, le mythe diffuse toute la force de sa magie ; il devient cosmos, univers.

nismen sind Feinde des Körpers.« Gilles Deleuze, in *Francis Bacon, Logik der Empfindung*, kommentiert: »Der Körper ohne Organ ... das ist ein starker, gestärkter Körper ... Die Gestalt, sie ist eben der Körper ohne Organ ... Das Fleisch ist jener Körperzustand, in dem lebendes Fleisch und Knochen eins werden ... Das Fleisch ist kein totes Fleisch, es hat alle Leiden bewahrt ... Bacon sagt nicht »Mitleid mit den Tieren«, er sagt vielmehr, daß jeder Mensch, der leidet, aus Fleisch ist. Fleisch haben Mensch und Tier gemeinsam ... Der Maler ist Metzger ...« Deleuze zitiert sodann Bacon selbst: »Mich haben stets Bilder berührt, die sich mit Schlachthäusern und Fleisch befassen; sie stehen für mich in engem Zusammenhang mit allem, was Kreuzigung ist. Es steht fest, daß wir Fleisch sind, wir sind schon künftige Gerippe. Wenn ich zu einem Metzger gehe, überrascht mich stets, dort nicht selbst anstelle des Tiers zu sein.« Deleuze sagt es deutlich: »Der Mensch ist ein Tier, wenn er leidet, das Tier ist ein Mensch, wenn es leidet. Das ist die Realität des Werdens. Welcher Mensch, der in Kunst, Politik, Religion oder anderweitig neue Wege geht, hat nicht diesen besonderen Augenblick erlebt, in dem er nur noch Tier war und nicht für die Kälber, sondern vor den Kälbern, die sterben müssen, verantwortlich wurde.« Welche Nähe zwischen der philosophischen Lesart des Werkes eines großen Malers in unserem Jahrhundert und unserem Empfinden angesichts der *Schlachthof*-Bilder Ennadres, der im übrigen sein Selbstbildnis mit einem Phantasieumriß seiner Gestalt auf einen Fleischhaufen projiziert hat. Es wäre wirklich töricht, sich nach der Ähnlichkeit zu fragen, wo ganz klar ist wie für Deleuze: »Der Fleisch-Kopf ist die Tier-Werdung des Menschen.«

Ennadre geht niemals illustrierend, erzählend oder symbolisch, sondern gestalterisch vor; »die Gestalt befreien«, »die Gestalt aus dem Symbolischen herauslösen« – alles Ausdrücke von Deleuze, die den Sinn seines Vorgehens angemessen wiedergeben. Wenn sich seine Bilder manchmal der Abstraktion nähern, so ist das niemals ihr Endstadium, denn er verfolgt Gestalt und Empfindung, die von Gewalt ausgelöst werden: »Was mich interessiert, ist das, was hinter dem Motiv liegt, Geburt, Tod, um von Gewalt loszukommen. Massaker und Barbarei habe ich zu Genüge in Schlachthöfen gesehen. Diese scheußliche Gewalt versucht mein Licht zu sühnen, es zeigt deshalb den Schrecken im Angesicht dieser Gewalt, keine Schauszenen des Horrors, die sie hervorbringt.« Erlebte Gewalt in der Erinnerung wiederfinden, sich ihr überall nähern, wo er sie wahrnimmt, um uns von ihr zu entfernen und sie auszutreiben, indem er »das Gefühl von Gewaltlosigkeit auslöst«. Und Deleuze zieht folgenden Schluß: »Der Gewalt des Dargestellten (des Sensationellen, des Klischeehaften) steht die Gewalt der Empfindung gegenüber. Diese wirkt unmittelbar auf das Nervensystem, über verschiedene Ebenen und Bereiche, die sie durchläuft: Ihre Gestalt hat nichts von der Beschaffenheit eines abgebildeten Gegenstands. So auch bei Artaud: Grausamkeit ist nicht, was man dafür hält, und sie hängt immer weniger von dem ab, was dargestellt ist.«

Die Exhumierten aus Herculaneum (1985-90) haben etwas von der Schönheit einer Auferstehung. Ennadre photographiert dort nicht die Toten, son-

myself. I'm a hanged man". There is no hint of melodrama here: Ennadre is neither suicidal nor a murderer, merely a hanged man who lives, eats, drinks and works and is condemned to death like the rest of us, but reinterprets his death-sentence every time he prints a negative. In the image, the hanged man is no longer there; all that remains is his imprint on the wall, blurred by time: traces, incrustations, lines, diffuse forms, stretched from top to bottom, from black to white, by the shadow of the rope. Its splendour is that of a sublimated fantasy. This humility, astonishing for a contemporary artist, should not deceive us; it shows that Ennadre is not content with vainglory, but shares in the greatest of ambitions, to live up to art itself, and, above all, to go beyond himself.

In 1989, Ennadre selected one or two *Gravestones and Paving Stones from the Medina in Fez.* Fez is a town swarming with craftsmen at work and alleys in which the houses are closed, a sunlit hill where the dead watch over the living. The depths of time in a sculpted wooden door, overflowing with history and radiating its own "aura". Gravestones where the Arab calligraphy, so beautiful it leaves you speechless, traces out the secrets of its unmoving message.

Lascaux (1990) led Ennadre to ponder the meaning of intuitively with his eyes. The depth of the shadows, when linked with the clarity of his gaze, denounces the role played by the sacred in these caves. The spells and magic known to be characteristic of the world of the hunt are above all a way of exorcising the death inflicted on the animal. Bataille, the author of *Lascaux, or the Birth of Art,* is not far off; Bataille, who once wrote in *Eroticism*: "Lascaux, where a dying bison confronts the man who may have killed him, whom the painter has given the appearance of a dead man. The subject . . . would be murder or expiation".

Ennadre is haunted by a desire to return to the origin and genesis of the human venture, even though, as he knows, any attempt at satisfying that desire is vain. No matter: the tragic is at the heart of his *Paleontological Traces* (1991), where, remote from any earthly paradise, the traces of the first men emerge in a chaos of bones and trembling earth animated by the luminous spirals of myth: the image dreams. . . .

Like a Renaissance artist, in 1991 Ennadre was commissioned by the French Caisse des Monuments Historique to work on a book on Notre-Dame de Paris. He had never visited the monument and was as ignorant of Catholicism as he was of the Muslim religion. This makes his visual approach all the more striking, as though a kind of cultural unconscious had been at work in him. When Eve offers Adam the fruit of the tree of the knowledge of good and evil, Adam stands bathed in light, while Eve has been veiled by a touch of shadow from beneath the contact printer: Ennadre, unaware of what he was doing, has made her face almost black. In a

Plus l'œuvre est mythogène, plus grande est sa force mythologique, plus l'individu Ennadre se cache, plus sa présence s'éclipse : il aimerait disparaître complètement dans son œuvre, s'y dissoudre, parce qu'alors elle n'aurait plus besoin de lui, existerait dans l'évidence de son universalité, affranchie de son géniteur. Ainsi aurait-il retrouvé le statut de l'artiste : non un ego survalorisé, une vedette, mais un simple support absent, une circonstance inutile, un sujet dans le sens premier du mot : « celui qui est dessous », au degré zéro, et qui cède le pas devant la forme, la Figure, la substance et la puissance mythologique de l'œuvre existant enfin, autonome par la seule fonction symbolique qu'elle exerce. Cette volonté de disparaître, ce désir de s'abolir et de s'ensevelir dans l'œuvre, Ennadre l'exprime avec une particulière acuité dans *L'Empreinte du pendu* (1987), qu'il appelle parfois *Autoportrait II* : « Arriver à être zéro ... n'y être plus que pour rien ... me supprimer ... je suis un pendu. » Pas l'ombre d'un mélodrame ici : Ennadre n'est ni suicidaire ni meurtrier, mais un simple pendu qui vit, mange et boit, travaille, un condamné à mort, comme nous tous, mais qui à chaque cliché réinterprète sa condamnation. Dans l'image, le pendu n'est plus là ; seule reste son empreinte sur le mur, estompée par le temps : traces, incrustations, lignes et formes diffuses tirées de bas en haut, du noir au blanc, par l'ombre de la corde. Splendeur du fantasme sublimé. Cette humilité, étonnante chez un artiste contemporain, ne nous abusera pas ; elle montre qu'Ennadre ne se satisfait pas de gloriole, mais participe de la plus grande des ambitions, être à la hauteur de l'art, même, et surtout, au-delà de lui-même.

En 1989, à Fès, ville grouillante de ruelles aux maisons fermées, d'artisans au travail, colline ensoleillée des morts qui veillent sur les vivants, Ennadre a retenu quelques *Pierres tombales et pavés de la médina de Fès*. L'épaisseur du temps dans une porte en bois sculpté, pleine d'histoire et chargée d'« aura ». Pierres tombales où l'écriture arabe calligraphiée, belle à en perdre la voix, dessine les secrets de son message immobile.

Les Fresques de Lascaux (1990) l'ont conduit à s'interroger sur leur sens, intuitivement, avec les yeux. La profondeur des ombres, jointe à la clarté de son regard, stigmatise le sacré qui règne dans ces cavernes. Sortilèges et magie propres au monde de la chasse, sait-on, mais surtout conjuration de la mort infligée à l'animal. Georges Bataille, auteur d'un *Lascaux ou la Naissance de l'art*, n'est pas loin, lui qui, dans *L'Erotisme*, écrivait : « Lascaux où un bison mourant affronte l'homme qui peut-être l'a tué auquel le peintre a donné l'aspect d'un mort. Le sujet ... serait le meurtre ou l'expiation. »

Le désir de retrouver l'origine et la genèse de l'aventure humaine hante Ennadre, bien que, et il le sait, toute tentative de le satisfaire soit vaine. Qu'importe, le tragique sera au cœur de ses *Vestiges paléontologiques* (1991), où, à mille lieues d'un paradis terrestre, les traces des premiers hommes prennent forme dans un chaos d'os

dern genau den Augenblick, in dem der Archäologe sie zuletzt aus der Vulkanlava befreit. Im Museum sind sie bald nur noch aufgereihte, gesäuberte und klassifizierte Knochen. Aber in dem Moment, in dem man sie freilegt, taucht eine Erinnerung auf. Lichthelle Skelette erinnern sich an das Entsetzen, das sie der Erde mitteilten. Sie haben sich seit fast 2000 Jahren, seit dem Tag ihrer Verschüttung, nicht gerührt. Ihre Wiederkehr schien undenkbar, es ist, als sei die Zeit stehengeblieben, als hätte der Tod am Ende die Partie verloren, als wäre die Geschichte aufgehoben. Ewige Wiederkehr, Triumph nicht des Todes, Triumph der Erinnerung. Indem das Werk die Zeit derart herausfordert, verweist es auf den Mythos, wo genau wie hier phantastische Bilder entstehen, um die Geheimnisse der Welt zu erklären. Der Mythos verwandelt auf wunderbare Weise diesen kleinen, fast skelettartigen Körper – halb Schatten, halb Schattenriß – der anfängt, sich aus dem Grab herauszuschälen, erschüttert von den Strahlen einer Begräbnissonne. In Ennadres Ikonen breitet der Mythos die ganze Kraft seines Zaubers aus; er wird zum Kosmos, zum Universum.

Je trächtiger das Werk an Mythen ist, umso größer ist seine mythologische Kraft, umso mehr verbirgt sich das Individuum Ennadre, umso mehr entfernt es sich: Gerne würde er vollkommen aus seinem Werk verschwinden, sich auflösen. Dann bedürfte es seiner nicht mehr, wäre es offensichtlich universal, wäre es von seinem Schöpfer befreit. Auf diese Weise hätte er den Status des Künstlers erreicht: Kein überbewertetes Ego, kein Star, nur ein einfacher, abwesender Halt, ein unnötiger Umstand, ein Subjekt in der ursprünglichen Bedeutung des Wortes: ›der, der darunter ist‹. Auf dem Nullpunkt, der der Form den Vortritt gibt, d.h. der Gestalt, der Substanz und der mythologischen Kraft des Werkes, das schließlich existiert und allein durch die symbolische Funktion, die es ausübt, autonom ist. Ennadre drückt diesen Willen zu verschwinden, diesen Wunsch, sich abzuschaffen und sich im Werk zu begraben, mit besonderer Schärfe im *Abdruck des Erhängten* aus (1987), den er manchmal *Selbstporträt II* nennt: »Dahin kommen, nicht zu sein ... darin nur noch für nichts zu sein ... mich abschaffen ... ich bin ein Erhängter.« Nicht der Schatten eines Melodrams darin: Ennadre ist weder lebensmüde noch Mörder, nur ein einfacher Erhängter, der lebt, ißt, trinkt und arbeitet, ein zum Tode Verurteilter wie wir alle, der aber bei jedem Negativ seine Verurteilung neu interpretiert. Der Erhängte ist nicht mehr im Bild; übrig ist nur sein mit der Zeit verblaßter Abdruck an der Wand: Spuren, Ablagerungen, vom Schatten des Stricks verschwommene Linien und Formen, die von unten nach oben vom Schwarz bis zum Weiß verlaufen. Glanzstück eines verklärten Phantasmas. Diese Bescheidenheit, die bei einem zeitgenössischen Künstler überrascht, führt uns nicht auf eine falsche Fährte; sie zeigt, daß Ennadre nicht nach Ruhm strebt, sondern die größte aller Ambitionen hegt, nämlich auf der Höhe der Kunst zu sein, sie vor allem über sich hinauswachsen zu lassen.

1989 hat Ennadre in Fès, der Stadt des Sträßchengewimmels, mit verschlossenen Häusern und Handwerkern bei der Arbeit, vom sonnenüberfluteten Hügel der Toten, die über die Lebenden wachen,

painting on the wall, the long pipe of the cleaning lady's hoover might remind one of the spear with which the Roman soldier pierced the side of Christ. In another image, death, reduced to the undulating fabrics in which its skeleton is wrapped, shows only the bones of its hand. Ennadre's imagination confines itself to what he has noticed about the cathedral. He has his own way of framing details, and fixes his vision, piece by piece, using much the same method as butchers use to cut up lamb in the medina. The monument is portioned up into blocks of light and close-ups.

Ennadre went to Auschwitz in 1992. An inner necessity drove him to visit the place where horror and barbarity reached fever pitch, and where, often as not, the treachery of words and images proves unbearable. Under the circumstances, any suggestion of the aesthetic would be enough to give you the shivers. Ennadre looked respectfully at the historical photographs in which memory is enshrined, inscribing on film only his impression of contemporary horror. No general view of the camp and barracks, no montage of images from the time, only close-ups that are like cries: of shoes, saucepans, numbered luggage, the names and origins of Jews referred to in this way. They were remains that Ennadre photographed, living traces that tell us that the extermination will never be forgotten. These everyday objects are the definitive faces of all those who were gassed, and the oven, seen in its true colours, is a denunciation of the premeditation of industrial and organised crime. They are images of remembrance that are non-descriptive, the stuff of absolute evil, at once indelible, accusing and expiatory.

In his pursuit of birth and death, whenever Ennadre is lucky enough to meet some distant ancestor, some elder brother in humanity, he is incapable of resisting. In 1992, on learning that "the ice man", who lived on the earth in the stone age, had just been discovered in South Tyrol, he immediately went to visit him, incorporating him in his gallery of anonymous portraits of stars who have patiently awaited their day of glory, like the dead exhumed at Herculaneum. Ennadre reforms his ancestor, thereby informing us about the being and emptiness of human time. The body with its mummified flesh is lit up by the outstretched arm and the light emanating from the fist: one senses a will that is petrified and definitive, as it were, a kind of challenge thrown up by time immemorial.

In *Squid and Fish* (1992-93), all the light comes from the bulging eyes of the fish, as though in suffocating they had taken the world's breath away. The thousand tentacular arms of the entwined octopuses are dancing, the graceful and majestic undulations of their whites-grays-blacks the final act of a tragic ballet.

Between 1993 and 1995, Ennadre went to Benin and Haiti to pin down on film another form of extreme transition in which the body all but dissolves, all but implodes or explodes in attempting

et de terre tremblée animé par les tourbillons lumineux du mythe : l'image rêve …

Comme au temps de la Renaissance, Ennadre a reçu en 1991 une commande de la Caisse des monuments historiques pour faire un livre sur *Notre-Dame de Paris*. Il n'était jamais entré dans ce monument, ignorait tout du catholicisme, comme d'ailleurs de la religion musulmane. Son angle de vue n'en est que plus saisissant, comme si une sorte d'inconscient culturel opérait en lui. Lorsqu'Eve tend à Adam le fruit de l'arbre de la connaissance du bien et du mal, Adam resplendit en pleine lumière alors qu'Ennadre, ignorant de ce qu'il fait, voile Eve, d'un coup d'ombre sous la tireuse : son visage est presque noir. Sur une toile accrochée au mur, le long tuyau de l'aspirateur de l'employé qui fait le ménage peut faire penser à la lance de l'officier romain qui transperce le Christ. Dans une autre image, la mort, réduite à un mouvement d'étoffes qui enveloppe son squelette, ne montre que les os de sa main. L'imaginaire d'Ennadre s'inscrit dans ce qu'il a retenu de la cathédrale. Il cadre les détails à sa manière, et fixe ses visions, morceau après morceau, à la façon des bouchers de la médina qui découpent l'agneau. Le monument se morcelle en pans de lumière et vues rapprochées.

Ennadre est allé à Auschwitz en 1992. Une nécessité intérieure l'a poussé à se rendre dans le lieu paroxystique de l'horreur et de la barbarie, où les mots et les images, le plus souvent, trahissent de façon insupportable. De l'esthétisme, en la circonstance, ferait frémir. Ennadre regarde avec respect les clichés historiques qui gardent la mémoire et n'inscrit sur sa pellicule que son impression d'horreur contemporaine. Aucune vue générale sur le camp et ses baraquements, aucun montage d'images d'époque, mais des gros plans, comme des cris, sur les chaussures, les casseroles, les valises avec les numéros, les noms et l'origine des Juifs ainsi désignés. Ce sont des restes qu'Ennadre a photographiés, des traces vivantes qui disent que l'extermination restera inoubliable à jamais. Ces objets familiers sont les visages définitifs des gazés, et le four, tel qu'en lui-même, dénonce la préméditation industrielle et organisée du crime. Images de mémoire non descriptives, matières de mal absolu, ineffaçables, accusatrices, conjuratrices.

Dans sa quête de la naissance et de la mort, lorsqu'Ennadre a la chance de rencontrer un grand ancêtre, un vieux frère en humanité, il ne résiste pas. Apprend-il en 1992 que l'on vient de découvrir dans le Tyrol du sud *L'Homme des glaces*, habitant de notre terre pendant l'âge de pierre, il lui rend immédiatement visite et l'annexe à sa galerie de portraits anonymes de vedettes qui se sont donné le temps d'attendre leur jour de gloire, comme les morts exhumés de Herculaneum. Ennadre reforme son ancêtre, et par là nous informe sur l'être et le néant du temps humain. Le mouvement tendu du bras et la lumière du poing éclairent ce corps aux chairs momifiées : on sent comme une volonté pétrifiée et définitive, une sorte de défi venu de la nuit des temps.

einige *Grabsteine und Pflastersteine aus der Medina* festgehalten. Sichtbar wird die verdichtete Zeit an einer geschichtsträchtigen holzgeschnitzten Tür mit einer ›Aura‹. Grabsteine mit kunstvollen arabischen Schriftzeichen, von stupender Schönheit: Träger der Geheimnisse ihrer unerschütterlichen Botschaft.

Die Wandmalereien von *Lascaux* (1990) haben ihn mit den Augen intuitiv nach ihrem Sinn fragen lassen. Die Tiefe der Schatten, in Verbindung mit seinem klaren Blick, kennzeichnen die Weihe, die diesen Höhlen eigen ist. Zauberei und Magie, wohl aus der Welt der Jäger, vor allem aber Beschwörung des Todes, der dem Tier zugefügt wird. Georges Bataille, der Autor des Werkes *Lascaux oder der Ursprung der Kunst*, ist dem nahe, wenn er in *Die Erotik* schreibt: »Lascaux, wo ein sterbender Bison dem Menschen gegenübersteht, der ihn vielleicht getroffen und dem der Maler das Aussehen eines Toten verliehen hat. Das Motiv … wäre Tötung oder Sühne.«

Das Verlangen, Ursprung und Werdegang des menschlichen Abenteuers zurückzuverfolgen, läßt Ennadre keine Ruhe, wenn auch, wie er genau weiß, jede Bemühung vergeblich ist. Immerhin liegt etwas Tragisches in seinen *Paläontologischen Spuren* (1991), wo tausend Meilen von einem irdischen Paradies entfernt, die Spuren der ersten Menschen in einem Chaos von Knochen und aufgewühlter Erde, das lebendig wird vom Lichttaumel des Mythos, Gestalt annehmen: Das Bild träumt …

Wie zu Zeiten der Renaissance erhielt Ennadre 1991 von der Caisse des monuments historiques den Auftrag, ein Buch über Notre-Dame de Paris zu machen. Er hatte das Gebäude nie zuvor betreten, wußte vom Katholizismus so wenig wie auch vom Islam. Umso packender ist sein Blickwinkel, als wirke eine Art kultisches Unterbewußtsein in ihm. Wenn Eva Adam die Frucht vom Baum der Erkenntnis von Gut und Böse reicht, erstrahlt Adam in vollem Licht, während Ennadre – ohne zu wissen, was er tut – Eva bei der Entwicklung mit einem Schatten verhüllt: Ihr Gesicht ist fast schwarz. Bei der Photographie eines an der Wand hängenden Ölgemäldes erinnert der lange Stil des Staubwedels eines Angestellten beim Saubermachen an die Lanze des römischen Offiziers, die Christus durchbohrt. Auf einem anderen Bild zeigt der Tod, der auf eine sein Skelett umhüllende wehende Stoffbahn reduziert ist, nur die Knochen seiner Hand. Ennadres Vorstellungsgabe transformiert das, was er in der Kathedrale gesehen hat. Er schafft seinen Rahmen für die Details, fixiert seine Visionen, Stück um Stück, nach Art der Metzger der Medina, die ein Lamm zerlegen. Das Gebäude erfährt eine Aufteilung in Lichtbahnen und Nahansichten.

1992 war Ennadre in Auschwitz. Eine innere Notwendigkeit hat ihn dazu getrieben, die Hochburg des Grauens und der Barbarei zu betreten, in der die meisten Worte und Bilder auf unerträgliche Weise täuschen. Ästhetik würde in diesem Zusammenhang erschaudern lassen. Ennadre betrachtet respektvoll die historischen Bildvorlagen, die das Gedächtnis daran bewahren, und schreibt seinem Film nur seinen derzeitigen Eindruck des Entsetzens ein. Keine Gesamtansicht vom Lager und seinen Baracken, keine Montage von Bildern jener Zeit,

to escape from the self through dance, ecstacy, delirium or trance. His images of bodies beside themselves now become a moving panorama of spiritual shadows, forms and lights.

At the Alhambra, faced with all the pomp and magnificence, Ennadre shunned the postcard view and limited himself to a choice of quintessential shots. Of door-knockers, for example: you can no longer tell if the hand is made of iron or flesh. Ennadre is not interested in general views, only in details whose shadows and shafts of light focus the spirit, duration, emotional and historical resonance of the place, its beauty and genius.

Ay! mi Toro! You remember the Ennadre photographs called *Slaughterhouse*. In 1996, he made a variation on the theme after visiting the Féria at Arles. What caught his attention in the bull-fight was not the spectacle as such, the passes and the *mise-à-mort*, but the men's relationship with the mortally wounded bull. Ay! mi Toro! It is no longer the wholesale killing of animals in industrial slaughterhouses, but the quasi-religious carving-up of an animal that has just died in the arena: his flesh, in Ennadre's eyes, carries on fighting; hence a plastic exultation that is particularly accomplished. The beauty, the tension, the madness of the *corrida* transform the body of the victim into large blocks of meat which continue to elude the butcher's knife. For Ennadre, the last act in a bull-fight is performed, dancing, after the *mise-à-mort*. The realistic aspect of some of the *Slaughterhouse* series is here given a more formal twist that is at times abstract, lyrical and incantatory. Horns, eyes, flesh and bones merge together to form a visual apotheosis. The degree of accomplishment Ennadre achieves in this work reaches far back in his creative approach.

Leaving the reader to his or her sensations in Ennadre's world of shadows and light, let us consider a moment our own commotion, one we have felt from the very beginning and which has since deepened into the most luminous black, that black light that is the epicentre of Ennadre's work.

It is a powerful aesthetic emotion, a shock, but above all a dynamic reminder overflowing with energy and lucidity. The driving-force behind Ennadre's work is the desire, ceaselessly reaffirmed, to ward off violence, for violence is despicable and unworthy of man. And to do so by creating its opposite, beauty. Remote from any form of morbid celebration, drawing out beauty and substituting it for violence is a political act in the metaphysical sense of that term.

"You walk on the dead, Beauty, and care not what you do", sings Baudelaire's "Hymn to Beauty" in *Les Fleurs du mal*, which Ennadre interprets lens in hand – not like a telescopic rifle trained on a target to shoot down, but as though he was stroking that part of life that cannot, and must not, be massacred by man: their freedom. In the chaos of inhuman

Avec *Pêches et poulpes* (1992-93), toute la lumière sort des yeux exorbités des poissons, comme si leur étouffement coupait le souffle du monde. Les mille bras tentaculaires des poulpes enlacés dansent, amples mouvements de grâce et de majesté, blancs-gris-noirs, final d'un ballet tragique.

Au cours des années 1993-1995, Ennadre est allé au Bénin et à Haïti immobiliser une autre sorte de passage à la limite et de dissolution, implosion et explosion du corps, celle qui, à travers danses, extases, délire et *Transes*, cherche à sortir de soi-même. L'image des corps en état second se fait alors panorama en mouvement d'ombres, formes et lumières spirituelles.

A l'Alhambra, devant le faste et la magnificence, Ennadre a fui les cartes postales. Il se limite à un choix de clichés quintessentiels, des heurtoirs sur les portes, par exemple : on ne sait plus si la main est de fer ou de chair. Les vues générales ne l'intéressent pas, mais les détails, qui concentrent en eux-mêmes, par traits d'ombre et de lumière, l'esprit, la durée, l'épaisseur affective et historique du lieu, sa beauté, son génie.

Ay! mi toro! Vous vous rappellez les photographies d'Ennadre intitulées *Boucherie*. En 1996 il revient sur le thème et varie après un voyage à la Féria d'Arles. De la corrida, il ne retient pas le spectacle, les passes, ni la mise à mort mais le rapport des hommes avec le taurreau touché à mort. Ay! mi toro! Ce n'est plus la bête tuée en série dans les abattoirs industriels, mais le dépeçage quasi religieux d'un animal qui vient de mourir dans l'arène : sa chair, aux yeux d'Ennadre, continue son combat. D'où une exultation plastique particulièrement aboutie. La beauté, la tension, la folie de la corrida transforment le corps de la victime en grands pans de viande qui esquivent encore les couteaux des bouchers. Pour Ennadre, le dernier acte tauromachique se joue, se danse, après la mise à mort. L'aspect parfois réaliste des *Boucheries* s'éclipse ici devant des élaborations formelles, parfois abstraites, lyriques et incantatoires. Cornes, yeux, chairs et os mêlés composent des apothéoses visuelles. Ennadre atteint, dans ce travail, un point d'aboutissement qui remonte loin dans sa démarche créatrice.

Au moment de laisser notre lecteur à ses sensations, dans le monde d'ombres et de lumière d'Ennadre, arrêtons-nous, pour notre part, à la commotion que nous avons éprouvée dès le premier instant et qui est allée s'approfondissant jusqu'au noir le plus lumineux, la lumière noire d'Ennadre, épicentre de son œuvre. Emotion esthétique forte, choc, mais surtout rappel dynamique chargé d'énergie et de lucidité. La finalité de cette œuvre est le désir, sans cesse réaffirmé, de conjurer la violence odieuse, indigne de l'homme. Conjuration de la violence par la création de son contraire, la beauté. Loin de toute célébration morbide, l'extraction de cette beauté et sa substitution à la violence relève d'un acte politique, au sens métaphysique du terme.

dafür Großaufnahmen, wie Schreie, von Schuhen, Kochtöpfen, Koffern mit den Nummern, den Namen und der Herkunft der so gekennzeichneten Juden. Es sind Reste, die Ennadre photographiert hat, Überlebensreste, die sagen, daß die Ausrottung auf immer unvergeßlich bleibt. Diese persönlichen Gegenstände sind die eindeutigen Gesichter der Vergasten, und der Ofen, so, wie er dasteht, verrät das industrielle, vorsätzlich organisierte Verbrechen. Keine beschreibenden Gedächtnisbilder, sondern unauslöschliche, anklagende, beschwörende Elemente des absolut Bösen.

Wenn Ennadre auf seiner Suche nach Geburt und Tod gelegentlich das Glück hat, einem großen Vorfahr, einem alten Bruder des Menschengeschlechts zu begegnen, kann er nicht widerstehen. Kaum hatte er 1992 erfahren, daß man in Südtirol den *Menschen aus dem Eis* entdeckt hat, schon suchte er ihn auf und reihte ihn ein in die Galerie anonymer Porträts von Stars, die sich Zeit gelassen haben, auf ihren großen Tag zu warten wie die Exhumierten von Herculaneum. Ennadre gibt seinem Vorfahr neue Gestalt und informiert uns dabei über das Sein und das Nichts der Zeit des Menschen. Die angespannte Bewegung des Arms und das Licht auf der Faust erhellen den mumifizierten Körper: Man spürt so etwas wie einen versteinerten, endgültigen Willen, eine Art Herausforderung, die aus dem Dunkel der Zeiten kommt.

Bei *Tintenfisch und Fische* (1992-93) kommt alles Licht aus den hervorquellenden Augen der Tiere, als nähme ihr Erstickungstod der Welt den Atem. Die tausend Fangarme der verschlungenen Kraken tanzen mit weiten, anmutigen und majestätischen Bewegungen, weiß-grau-schwarz, den Schlußtanz eines tragischen Balletts.

In den Jahren 1993-95 hat Ennadre Bénin und Haiti besucht, um dort auf andere Art Grenz- und Auflösungserfahrung festzuhalten, die Implosion und Explosion des Körpers, der bei Tänzen, in Extase, im Delirium oder in Trancezuständen aus sich auszubrechen versucht. Das Bild von Körpern, die außer sich sind, wird bei ihm zu einem Panorama aus Schattenbewegungen, Formen und übersinnlichen Lichtwirkungen.

Angesichts der Pracht und Großartigkeit der Alhambra hat Ennadre Postkartenansichten verschmäht (1995). Er beschränkt sich auf eine Auswahl von essentiellen Motiven, etwa die Türklopfer an den Pforten: Man weiß nicht mehr, ob die Hand aus Eisen oder aus Fleisch ist. Ihn interessieren nicht die Gesamtansichten, sondern die Details, die durch Schatten- und Lichtlinien das Geistige, die Dauer, die affektive und historische Tiefe des Ortes, seine Schönheit und seinen Genius ausloten.

Ay! mi toro! Sie erinnern sich an Ennadres Aufnahmen mit dem Titel *Schlachthöfe*. 1996 greift er das Thema wieder auf und variiert es nach einer Fahrt zur Féria von Arles. Er bewahrt vom Stierkampf weder das Schauspiel noch die Gesten des Torero, noch die Tötung des Stiers. Ihn bewegt die Beziehung der Menschen zum tödlich verletzten Stier. Ay! mi toro! – das ist nicht mehr das serienmäßig in den industriellen Schlachthäusern getötete Tier, es ist das geradezu andächtig in Stücke zerlegte

violence, an "I-don't-know-what", a "next to nothing" remains hidden, like a shadow of love; you still have to notice and take hold of it: absolute black is alone capable of clarifying this still, small light that man has no right to extinguish, on pain of becoming more bestial than the wild beasts themselves. It is the overriding importance of this aim that gives Ennadre's project and images their unity. Just as light has a constant speed, everything in Ennadre's work is governed by a constant. We are in the presence, not of themes, but of variations on one and the same theme, death. But to limit oneself to this observation would be either too much or too little.

Ennadre is certainly part of that gigantic tradition which puts death at the heart of every artistic creation. The dance of the Maccabees, the tombs, an entire literature stretching from Montaigne to Bataille (to limit ourselves in history and geography) marks out the terrain: it is man's mortal condition that gives rise to artists. True, but too general: the main thing still remains to be said. Death, then. But which death? How and why? One will have noticed that, beginning with the hands isolated from the rest of the body as a way of expressing pain and the weight of time and death, all Ennadre's photographs after *Birth,* from *Slaughterhouse* to *Paleontological Traces,* have taken as their subject lives, whether animal or human, at the very moment of their death, as was suggested by the title of the exhibition "Live Death". What fascinates Ennadre is the passage, the extreme point, the moment of truth in which death is already there, though only just, and life has that very instant ceased to exist. He does everything he can to eternalize that moment, to extract its quintessence, to approach it, to enshrine its memory, though always with life in mind. "I find death and it brings me back to life". This explains why the mediation of birth was needed to lead Ennadre towards the elusive mystery of death's vital power.

"O mysterious death", proclaimed Rimbaud, who, with regard to man, asserted in "Sun and Flesh": "Yes, even after death, in the form of pale skeletons He can live, an insult to first beauty!" An assertion of this kind, irreligious in inspiration, forces the poet to create light in darkness. *A Season in Hell*: "I shall reveal all the mysteries: mysteries religious or natural, death, birth, future, past, cosmogony, void". As in our allusions to this or that painter, we are not indicating a resemblance here, a direct line of descent or identification, but merely suggesting an unconscious affinity, a vibration. In a completely different universe, after removing them from a context of apology that is foreign to Ennadre, who limits himself to the world of immanence, one can hear the echo of Bossuet's words when, speaking before the Grandes Assemblées at the Louvre, he marvelled: "It is a strange weakness of the human spirit that never should death be present to it, thought it is plainly visible on all sides and in a thousand divers forms". There is no need for Ennadre to believe in any sort of divine Providence to rekindle the strength of the human spirit and exorcise its "strange weakness".

« Tu marches sur des morts, Beauté, dont tu te moques », chantait l'Hymne à la Beauté de Baudelaire dans *Les Fleurs du mal,* qu'Ennadre interprète l'objectif à la main, non comme un fusil-à-lunette, viseur tendu vers la cible à abattre, mais comme une caresse sur la part de vie qui ne peut, ni ne doit, être massacrée par les hommes, leur liberté. Dans les affres de la violence inhumaine, demeure cependant caché un « je-ne-sais-quoi, un presque-rien », comme une ombre d'amour ; encore doit-on le voir et le saisir : seul, le noir absolu est capable d'éclairer cette petite lumière que l'homme n'a pas le droit d'éteindre, sous peine de devenir plus bête que les bêtes sauvages. Cette finalité majeure de l'œuvre confère leur unité au projet et aux images. De même que la lumière a une vitesse constante, on aimerait écrire que tout chez Ennadre est gouverné par une constante. Mieux que des thèmes, nous sommes en présence de variations sur un seul et même thème, la mort. Mais s'en tenir à cette constatation serait ou trop, ou trop peu. Ennadre s'inscrit, certes, dans la vaste tradition qui place la mort au cœur de toute création d'art. Les danses des macchabées, les tombeaux, toute une littérature qui va de Montaigne à Bataille, pour se limiter dans l'histoire et la géographie, balisent le terrain : la condition mortelle de l'homme engendre les artistes. Vrai, mais par trop général : l'essentiel reste à dire. La mort donc, mais laquelle, comment et pourquoi ?

On aura remarqué que, depuis les mains, isolées du corps pour exprimer la douleur, le poids du temps et la mort, toutes les photographies d'Ennadre après les *Accouchements*, des *Boucheries* aux *Vestiges paléontologiques*, prennent pour sujet des êtres, animaux ou humains, au moment précis où ils vivent leur mort, comme le suggérait le titre de l'exposition *La Mort vive*. Ce qui fascine Ennadre, c'est le passage, le point-limite, l'instant de vérité où la mort est juste déjà là alors que la vie vient juste de cesser d'y être. Tout faire pour éterniser ce moment, en extraire la quintessence, s'en approcher, en garder la mémoire, dans une intention de vie. « Je retrouve la mort et ça me fait renaître. » Ennadre exprime ainsi pourquoi la médiation de la naissance s'est imposée à lui pour le mener vers l'insaisissable mystère de la puissance vitale de la mort.
« O mort mystérieuse », lançait Rimbaud qui, à propos de l'homme, affirmait dans « Soleil et Chair » : « Oui, même après la mort, dans les squelettes pâles Il peut vivre, insultant la première beauté ! » Une telle avancée, d'inspiration irréligieuse, impose au poète de faire la lumière dans le noir, *Une Saison en enfer* : « Je vais dévoiler tous les mystères, mystères religieux ou naturels, mort, naissance, avenir, passé, cosmogonie, néant. »

Comme lorsque nous avons fait allusion à tel ou tel artiste, il ne s'agit pas de signaler ici une ressemblance, une filiation ou une identification, mais simplement de suggérer une affinité, inconsciente chez Ennadre, une vibration. Dans un tout autre univers, sorties de leur contexte apologétique étranger à Ennadre qui s'en tient au monde de l'immanence, on entend en écho les

Tier, nachdem es soeben in der Arena gestorben ist. Sein Fleisch führt in den Augen Ennadres seinen Kampf weiter. Daraus entsteht ›Exultat‹ bildnerischer Vollendung. Schönheit, Spannung und Wahnsinn des Stierkampfs verwandeln den Körper des Opfers in große Fleischbahnen, die noch immer den Messern der Metzger ausweichen. Für Ennadre wird der letzte Akt des Stierkampfes erst nach der Tötung gespielt und getanzt. Der mitunter realistische Aspekt der Schlachthöfe wird hier ausgeblendet durch formale, manchmal abstrakte, lyrische und beschwörende Gestaltung. Hörner, Augen, Fleisch und Knochen bilden vermischt visuelle Apotheosen. Ennadre kommt mit dieser Arbeit zu einem Ergebnis, das in seinem schöpferischen Werdegang eine lange Vorgeschichte hat.

Kommen wir nun selbst, wo wir unseren Leser seinen Empfindungen überlassen haben, zu der Erschütterung, die wir gleich zu Beginn empfunden haben und die beim lichtesten Schwarz, dem schwarzen Licht Ennadres, dem Epizentrum seines Werkes, immer tiefer wirkte: eine starke, ästhetische und schockartige Erregung, vor allem aber eine aktive Mahnung, die Kraft und Hellsichtigkeit verrät. Das Hauptanliegen in diesem Werk ist der unaufhörlich wiederholte Wunsch, die Schande der Gewalt zu beschwören, die menschenunwürdig ist. Beschwörung der Gewalt durch die Schaffung ihres Widerparts, der Schönheit. Fern aller morbiden Beweihräucherung hat das Herausstellen dieser Schönheit anstelle der Gewalt etwas von einem politischen Akt in der metaphysischen Bedeutung des Begriffs.

»Schönheit, du gehst über Leichen, die dir gleichgültig sind«, klang es in Baudelaires Hymne an die Schönheit in den *Fleurs du Mal.* Ennadre interpretiert sie mit dem Objektiv in der Hand, nicht wie bei einem Gewehr mit Zielfernrohr den Sucher auf das zu vernichtende Ziel gerichtet, sondern mit liebevoller Geste für den Anteil ihres Lebens, der von den Menschen nicht geschändet werden kann und darf, ihre Freiheit. In den Schrecken unmenschlicher Gewalt bleibt doch noch ein »Ich-weiß-nicht-Was, ein Fast-Nichts« gleich einer Schattenspur von Liebe verborgen; man muß sie allerdings sehen, sie zu fassen bekommen. Nur das absolute Schwarz vermag dieses kleine Licht zum Leuchten zu bringen, das der Mensch auszulöschen kein Recht hat, wenn er nicht tierischer als wilde Tiere werden will. Dieses Hauptanliegen des Werks bewirkt im Gesamtkonzept und Einzelbild die Einheitlichkeit. Man möchte schreiben: Gleich der Konstanten bei der Lichtgeschwindigkeit wird auch bei Ennadre alles von einer Konstanten beherrscht. Wir haben vor uns weniger verschiedene Themen als vielmehr Variationen über ein einziges Thema, den Tod. Doch bei dieser Feststellung stehenzubleiben, ist einerseits zu viel und zugleich zu wenig. Zwar gehört Ennadre in die breite Tradition derer, die den Tod ins Zentrum allen künstlerischen Schaffens stellen. In diesen Bereich sind Totentänze, Gräber, eine ganze Literatur von Montaigne bis Bataille Schwerpunkte, um nur bei Geschichte und Geographie zu bleiben. Die Todesbedingtheit des Menschen bringt den Künstler hervor – doch ist das viel zu allgemein; das Wesentliche bleibt dabei ausgespart. Der Tod, ja, aber welcher, wie und wann?

The image, then, concentrates all its energies – those of Ennadre, our own – and redirects them towards life: tensions, intensities, tragedy. No artifice, never any lighting from behind, only darkness and light, a counter-death. His world is inhabited by myth, the myth of origin and ends, of revival. The cosmic order demonstrates that indissociability of life and death that only a poetic vision can reveal.

So: is Ennadre a photographer or something else? It is a ludicrous question. He sculpts the light of catastrophes. His logic is that of a plastic artist who would found his work on the *Principles of an Aesthetic of Death*. He will pierce your eye to the brain in its very flesh.

Unique of its kind, Ennadre's work has a place among the very great. To see it is like listening to Mahlers *Kindertotenlieder* sung by Kathleen Ferrier.

paroles d'un Bossuet,lorsque, au Louvre, devant les grands assemblés, il s'étonnait: «C'est une étrange faiblesse de l'esprit humain que jamais la mort ne lui soit présente, quoiqu'elle se mette en vue de tous côtés et en mille formes diverses.» Point n'est besoin à Ennadre de croire à une quelconque Providence divine pour raviver la force de l'esprit humain et conjurer son «étrange faiblesse».

L'image ici concentre toutes les énergies, celle d'Ennadre, les nôtres, et les réoriente vers la vie: tensions, intensités, tragique. Aucun artifice, pas le moindre contre-jour, mais du noir, de la lumière, de la contre-mort. Ce monde est habité par le mythe, celui de l'origine et des fins, celui de la renaissance. L'ordre du cosmos manifeste l'indissociabilité de la vie et de la mort que seule une vision poétique peut dévoiler.

Alors, Ennadre, photographe ou autre chose ? Question dérisoire. Il sculpte la lumière des catastrophes. Sa logique est celle d'un plasticien qui s'appuierait sur les *Principes d'une esthétique de la mort*. Il vous percera l'œil jusqu'au cerveau, en pleine chair.

Unique en son genre, l'œuvre d'Ennadre a sa place parmi les plus grandes. La voir, c'est écouter les *Kindertotenlieder* de Mahler, avec la voix de Kathleen Ferrier.

Man wird bereits bemerkt haben, daß seit den vom Körper getrennten *Händen*, die Schmerz, Last der Zeit und den Tod zum Ausdruck bringen, alle Photographien Ennadres, nach *Geburt, Schlachthof*, bis zu den *Paläontologischen Spuren*, Tiere oder Menschen genau in dem Moment zum Motiv haben, in dem sie ihren Tod erleben – wie es auch eine frühere Ausstellung Ennadres, *La Mort vive*, zum Ausdruck brachte. Ennadre fesselt der Übergang, der Grenzfall, der Wahrheitsmoment, in dem der Tod schon da ist und das Leben gerade erlischt. Alles tun, um diesem Augenblick ewige Dauer zu verleihen, ihm das Wesentliche zu entnehmen, ihm nahezukommen, das Gedächtnis an ihn zu bewahren, um sich dem Leben damit zuzuwenden. »Ich sehe den Tod wiederkehren und werde wiedergeboren.« Ennadre sagt auf diese Weise, warum es ihm so wichtig geworden war, die Geburt ins Bild zu bringen, um zum unbegreiflichen Geheimnis der vitalen Kraft des Todes vorzudringen. »Oh, geheimnisvoller Tod«, rief Rimbaud aus, der im Blick auf den Menschen in ›Sonne und Fleisch‹ versicherte: »Ja, selbst nach dem Tode vermag Er in den bleichen Skeletten zu leben und der ursprünglichen Schönheit zu trotzen!« Solch gewagte, unreligiöse Haltung zwingt den Dichter, in *Eine Zeit in der Hölle* Licht in das Dunkel zu bringen: »Ich werde alle Mysterien enthüllen, ob religiösen oder natürlichen Ursprungs, Tod, Geburt, Zukunft, Vergangenheit, die Entstehung der Welt und des Nichts.«

Auch hier geht es, wie auch sonst, wo wir auf diesen oder jenen Künstler angespielt haben, nicht darum, auf Ähnlichkeit, Verwandtschaft oder Gleichartigkeit hinzuweisen; es soll nur die unbewußte Wesensverwandtschaft mit Ennadre, eine Schwingung, angedeutet werden. Aus einer ganz anderen Welt, aus einem Zusammenhang der Rechtfertigung, der Ennadre, der sich an die immanente Welt hält, fremd ist, hört man wie ein Echo die Worte Bossuets, die er im Louvre vor den großen Versammlungen erstaunt ausrief: »Es ist eine seltsame Schwäche des menschlichen Geistes, daß der Tod ihm nie gegenwärtig ist, wo er sich doch allseits und in tausenderlei verschiedenen Formen zeigt.« Ennadre hat keinerlei Bedürfnis, an irgendeine göttliche Vorsehung zu glauben, den menschlichen Geist zu beleben und seine »seltsame Schwäche« zu beschwören.

Das Bild eint alle Energien, die Ennadres wie auch unsere, und richtet sie wieder auf das Leben: Spannungen, Intensität, Tragisches. Nichts Künstliches, kein Gegenlicht, nur Schwarz, Licht, Gegen-Tod. In dieser Welt lebt der Mythos vom Ursprung und vom Ende, der Mythos der Wiedergeburt. Die Weltordnung zeigt, daß Leben und Tod untrennbar sind, was allein eine poetische Vision zu enthüllen vermag.

Ennadre – ein Photograph also oder etwas anderes? Eine alberne Frage. Er formt als Bildhauer das Unglückslicht. Seine Logik ist die eines Bildners, der sich auf die *Prinzipien einer Todesästhetik* stützen könnte. Er sticht einem ins Auge, bis ins Gehirn, mitten hinein ins Fleisch.

In seiner Einzigartigkeit hat das Werk Ennadres seinen Platz unter den größten. Es anschauen ist, als hörte man die *Kindertotenlieder* von Gustav Mahler, gesungen von Kathleen Ferrier.

HANDS, BACK, FEET

LES MAINS, LE DOS, LES PIEDS

HÄNDE, RÜCKEN, FÜSSE

1978–82

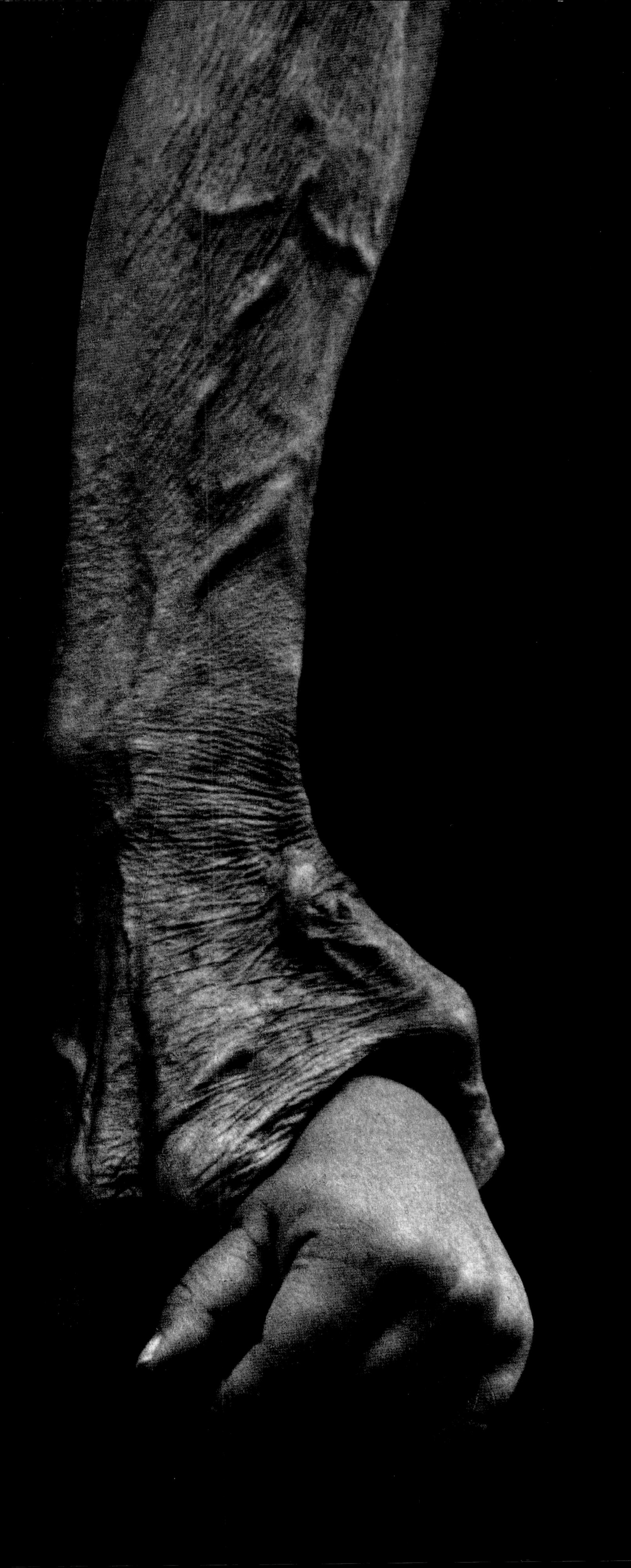

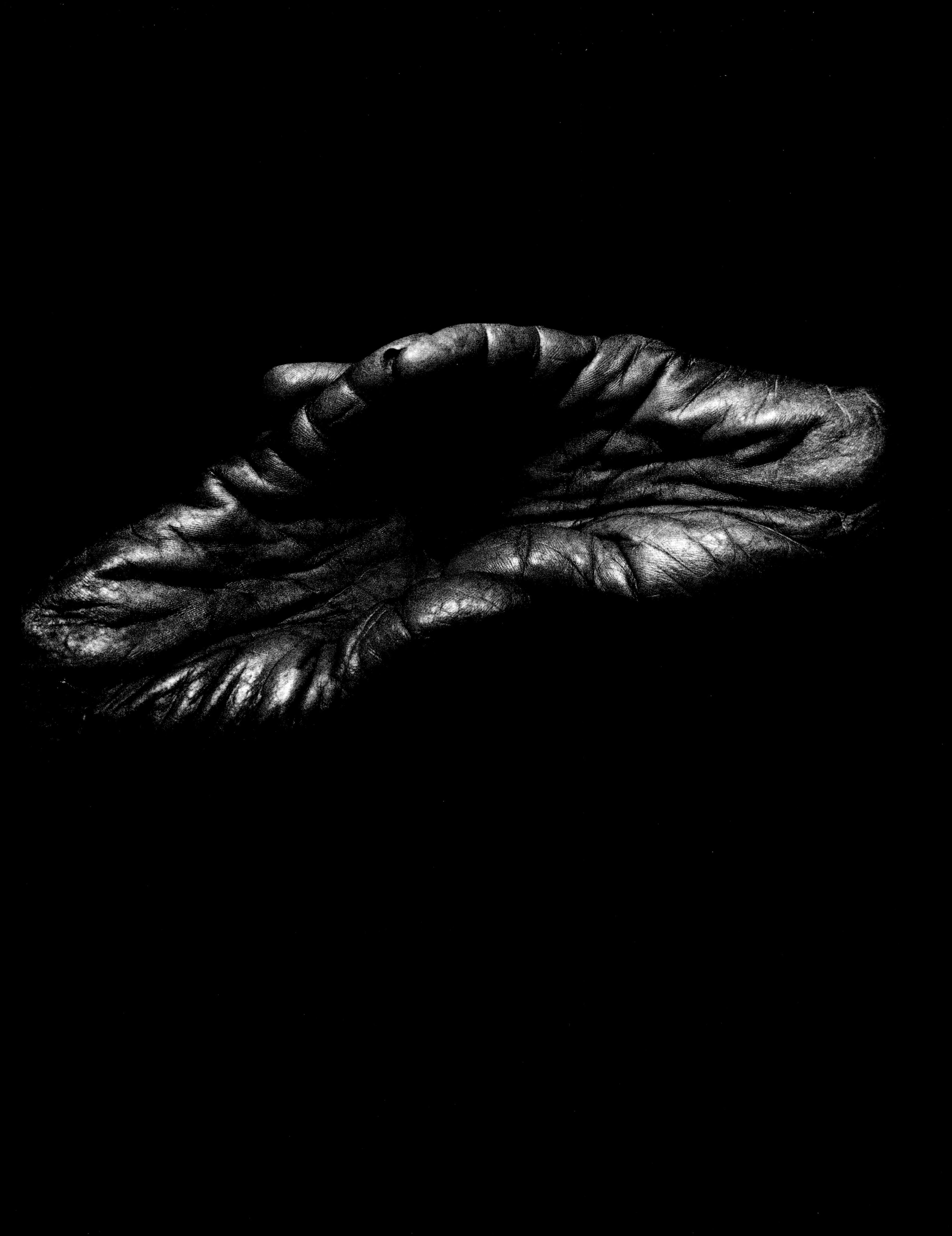

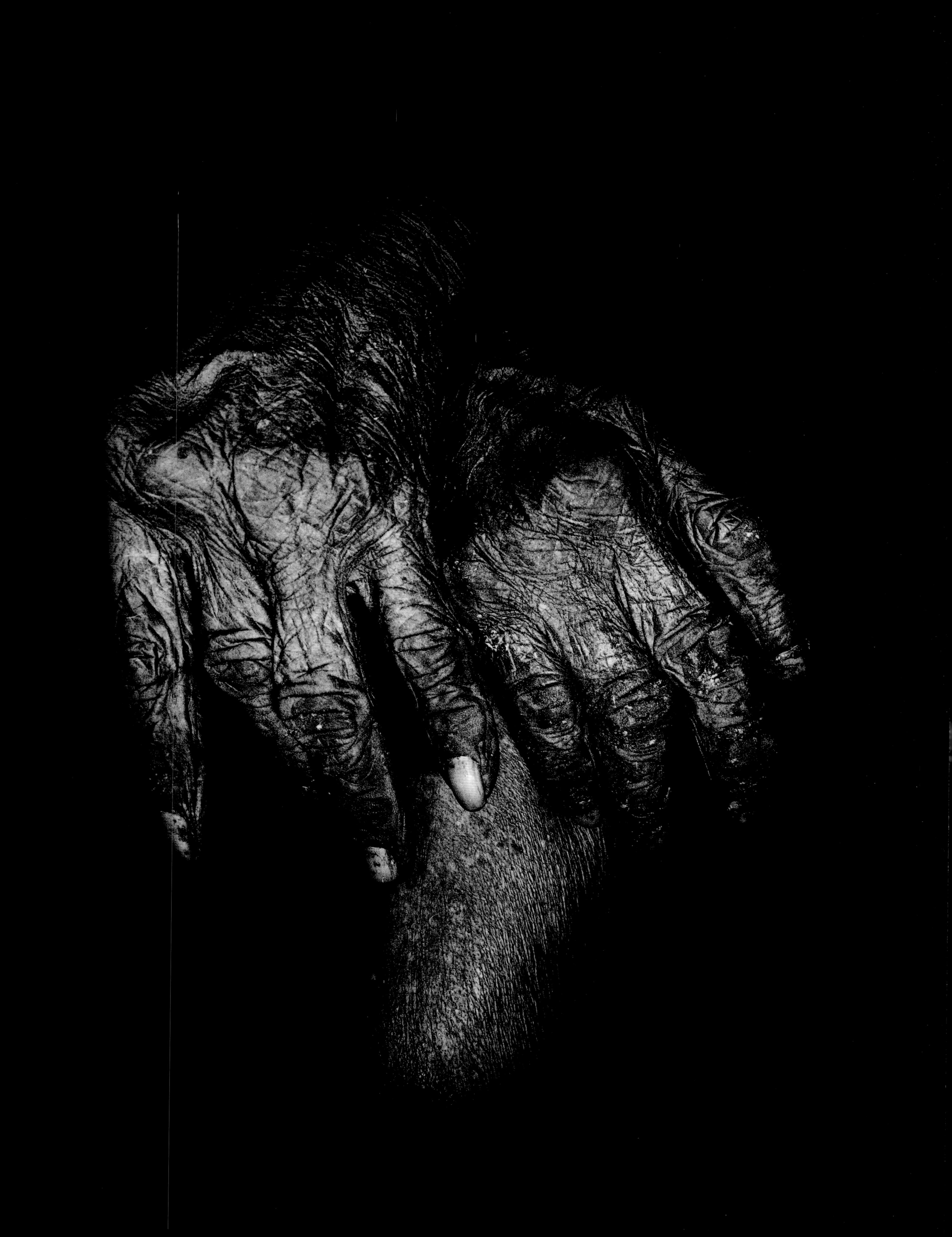

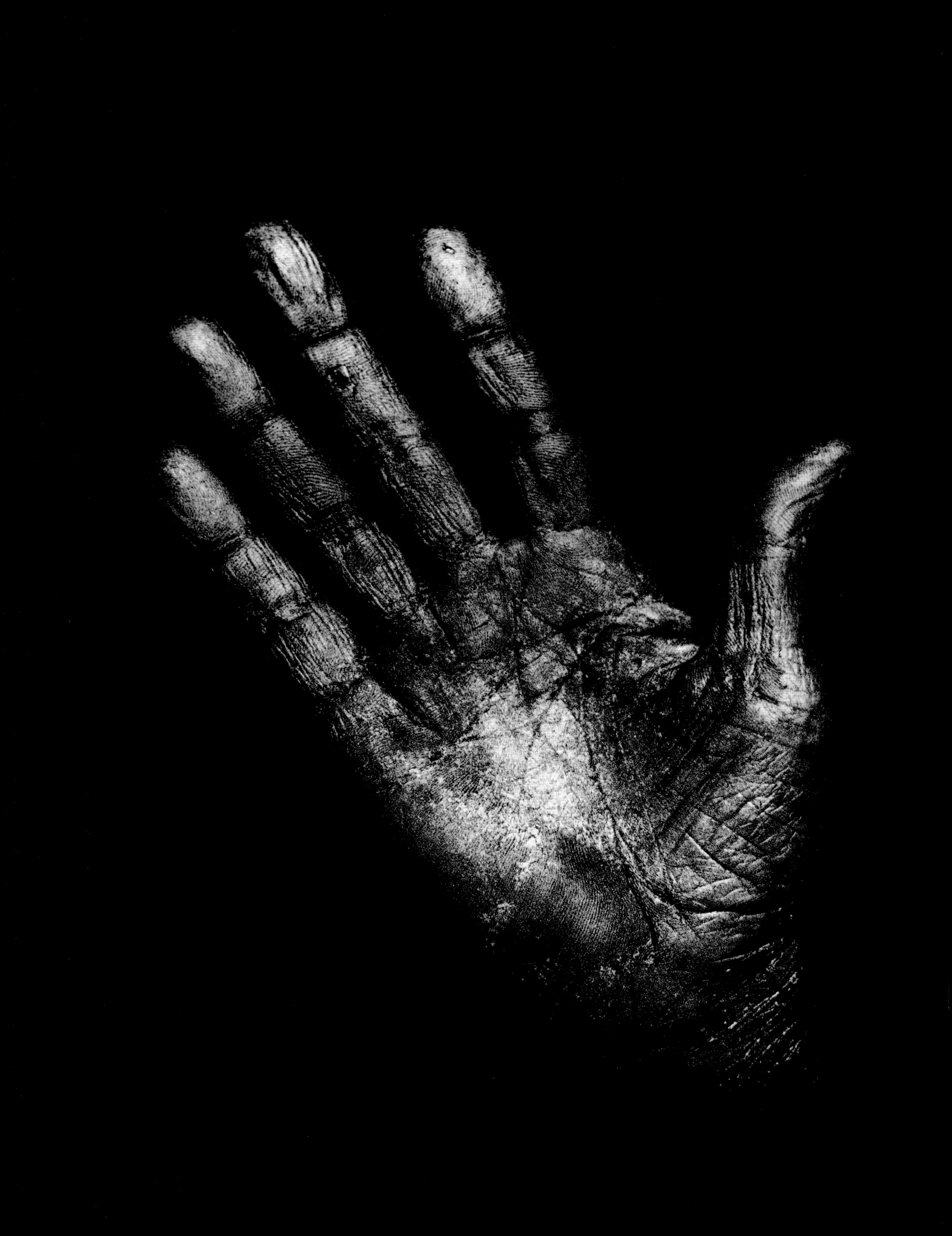

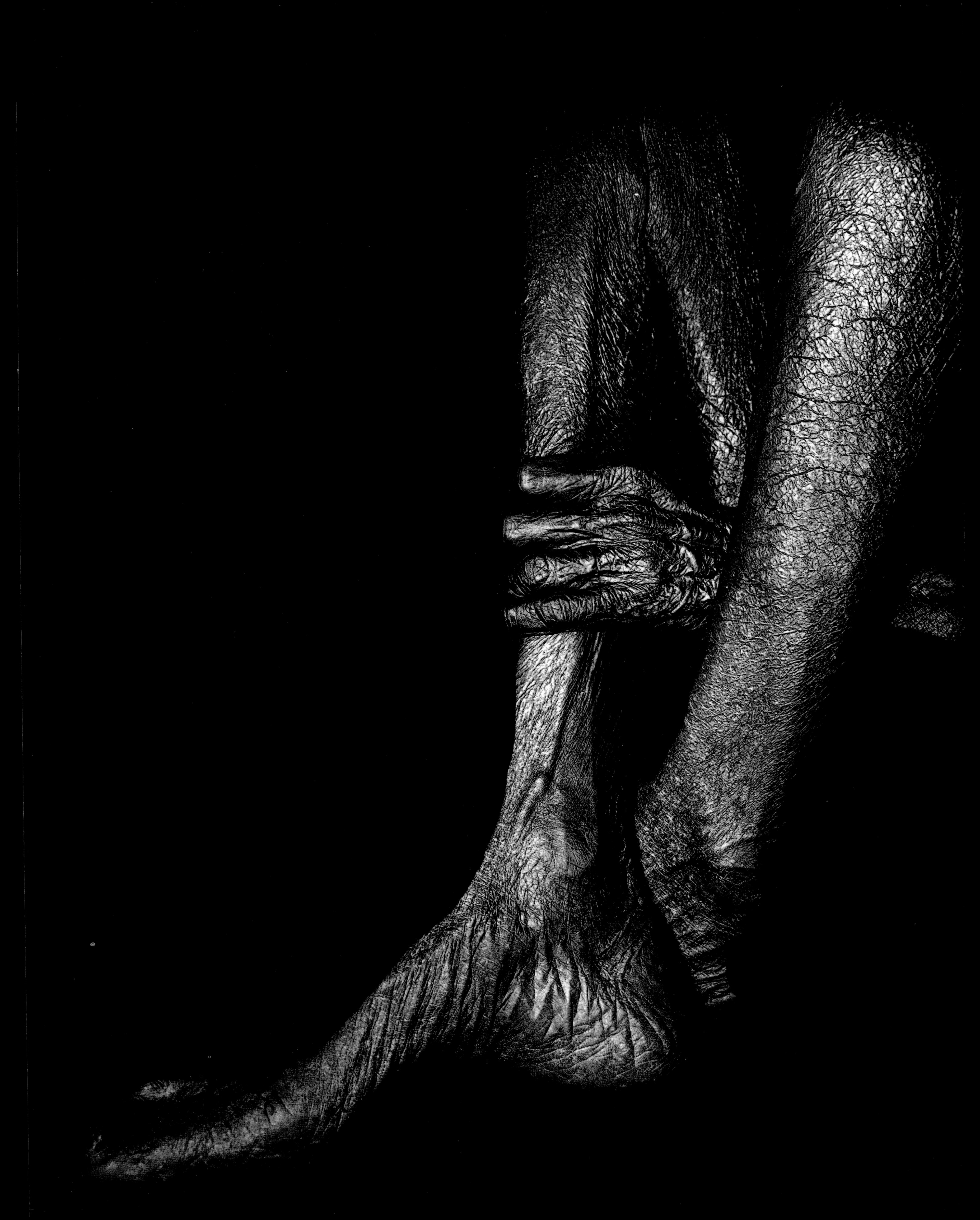

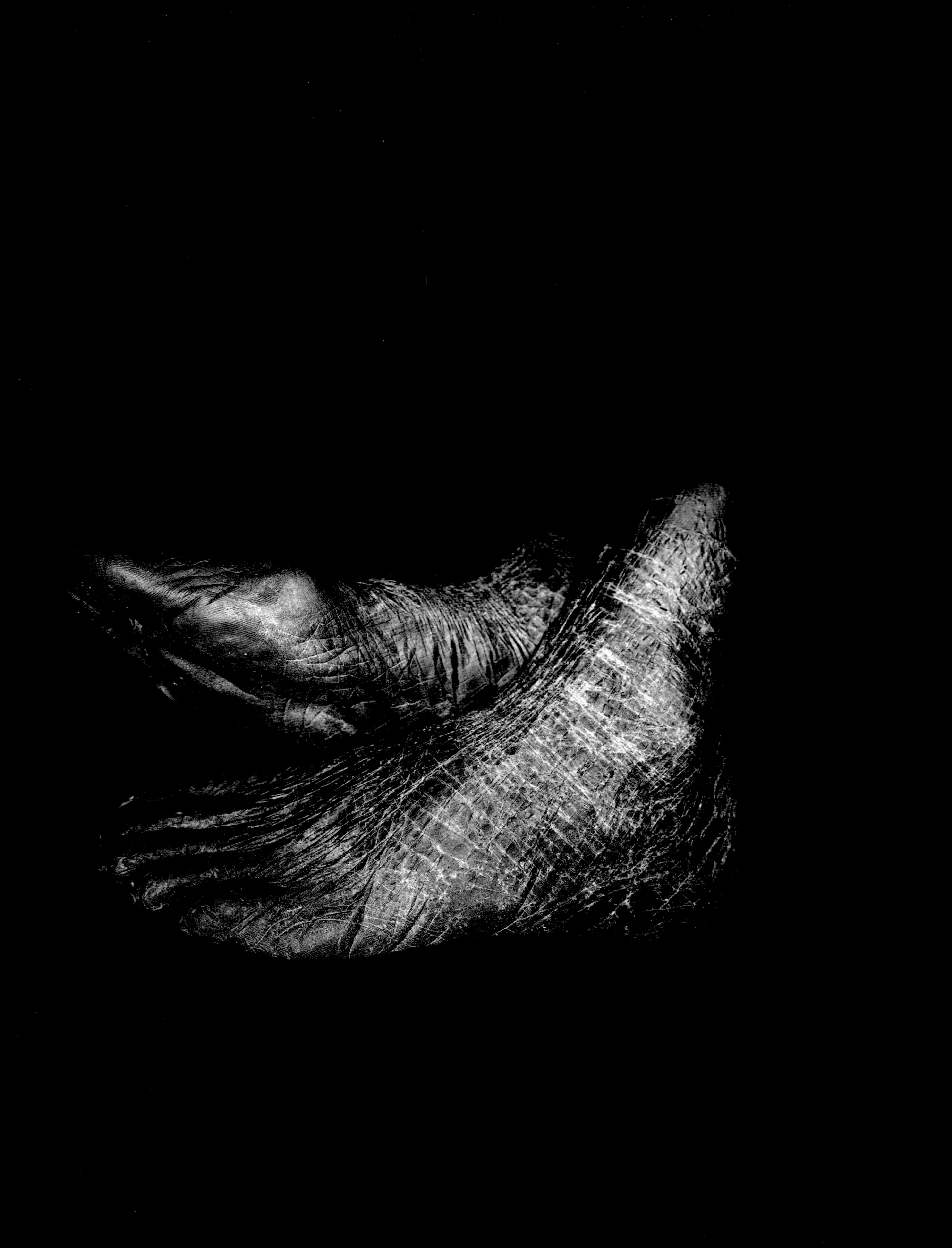

BIRTH

ACCOUCHEMENTS

GEBURT

1982–83

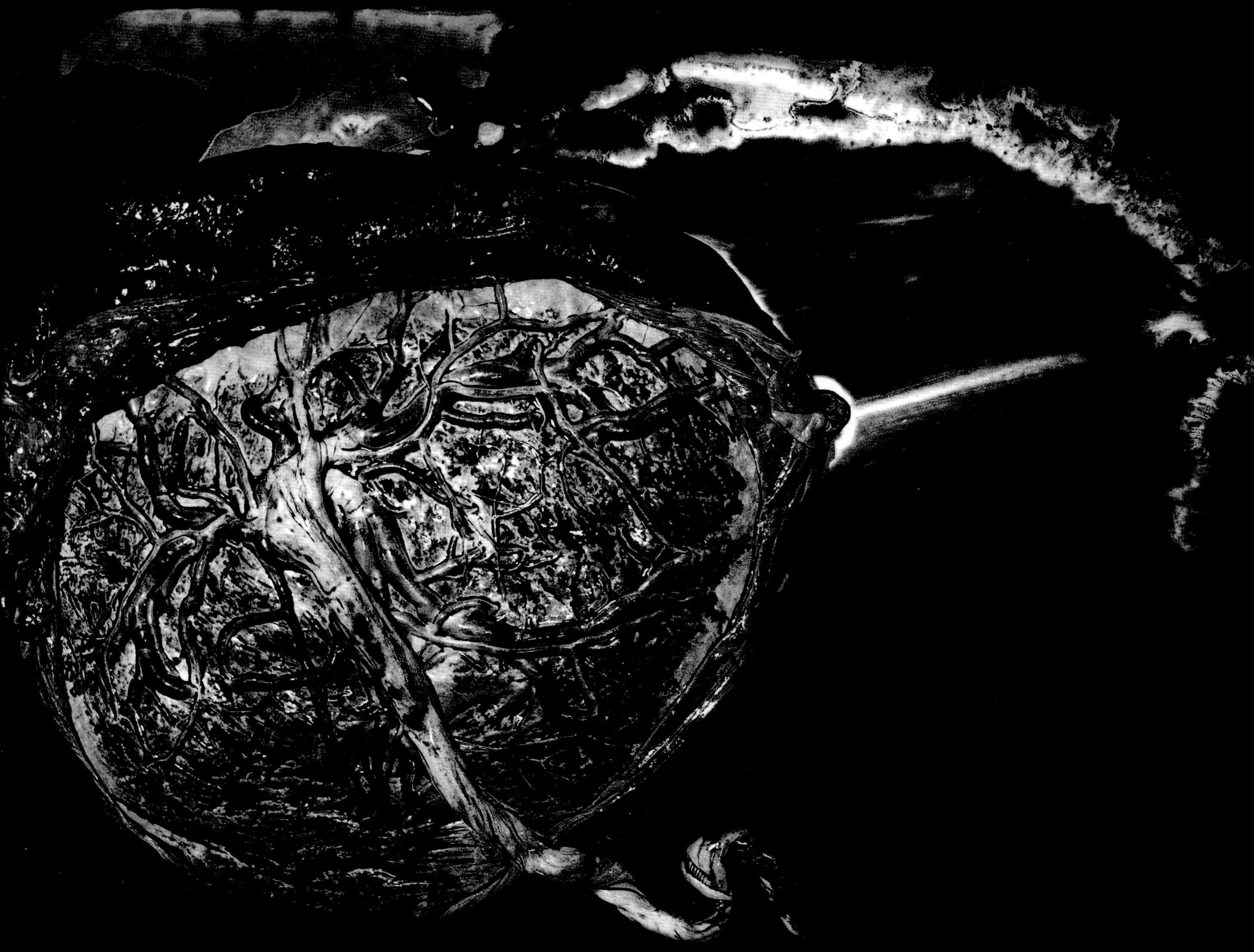

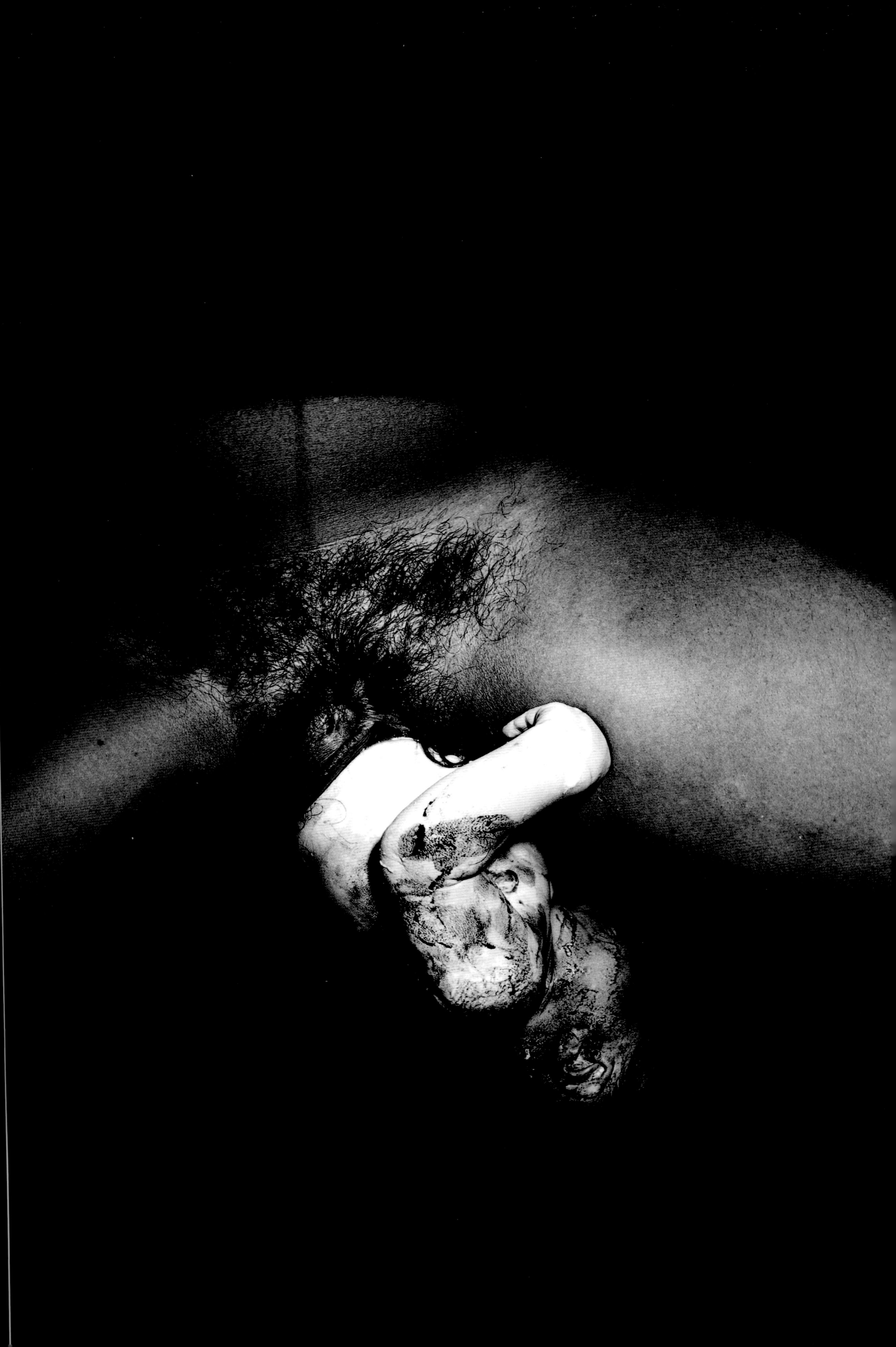

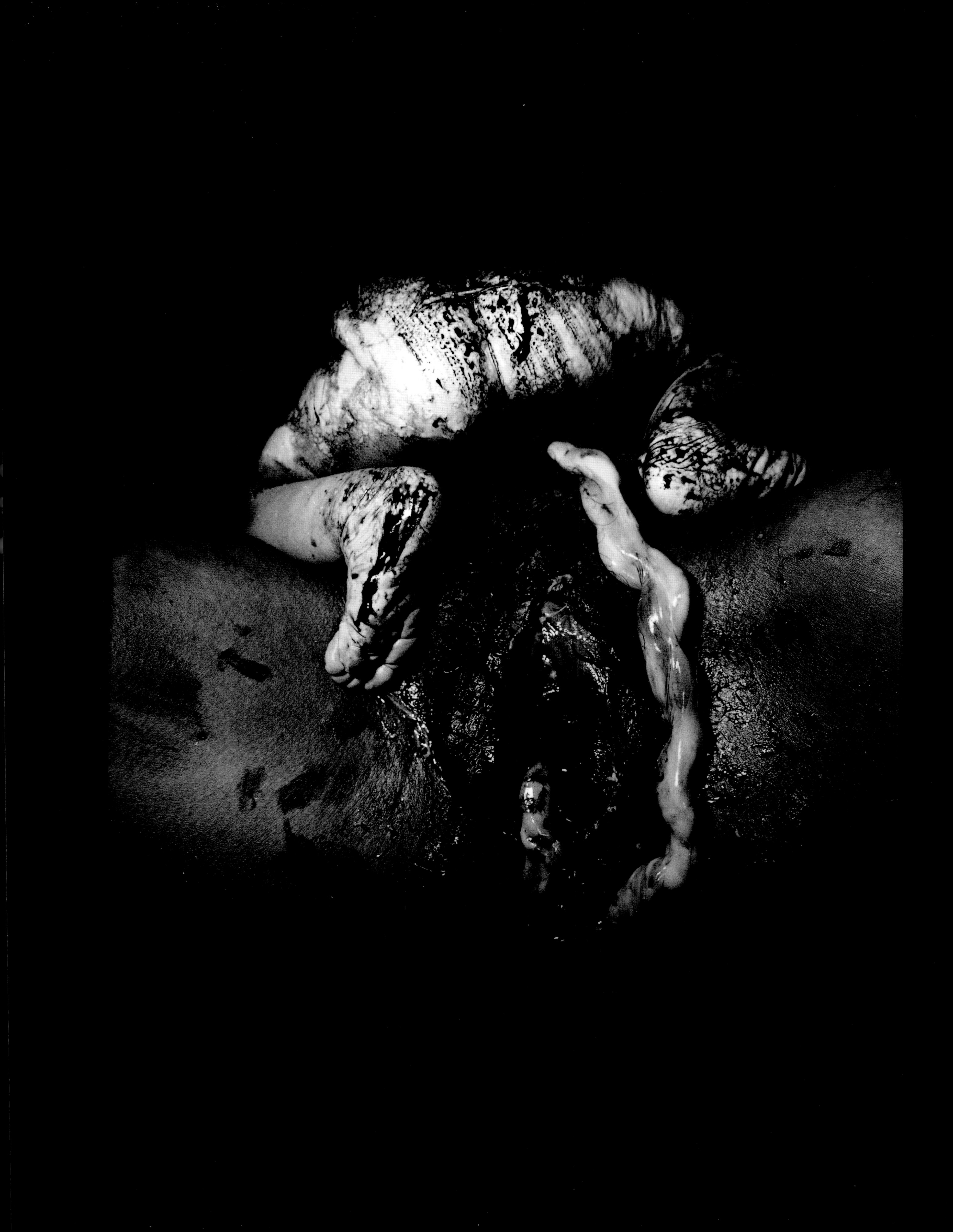

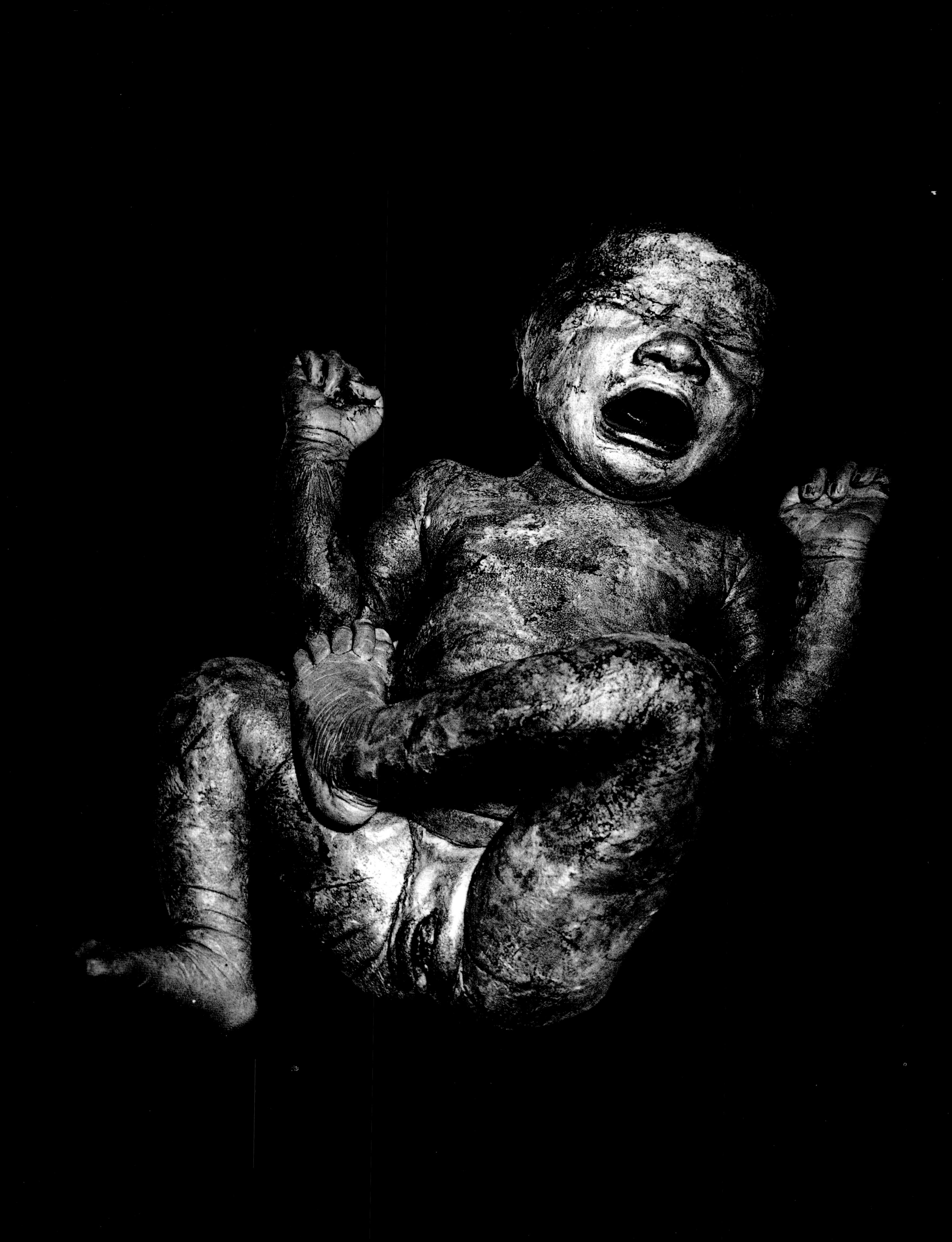

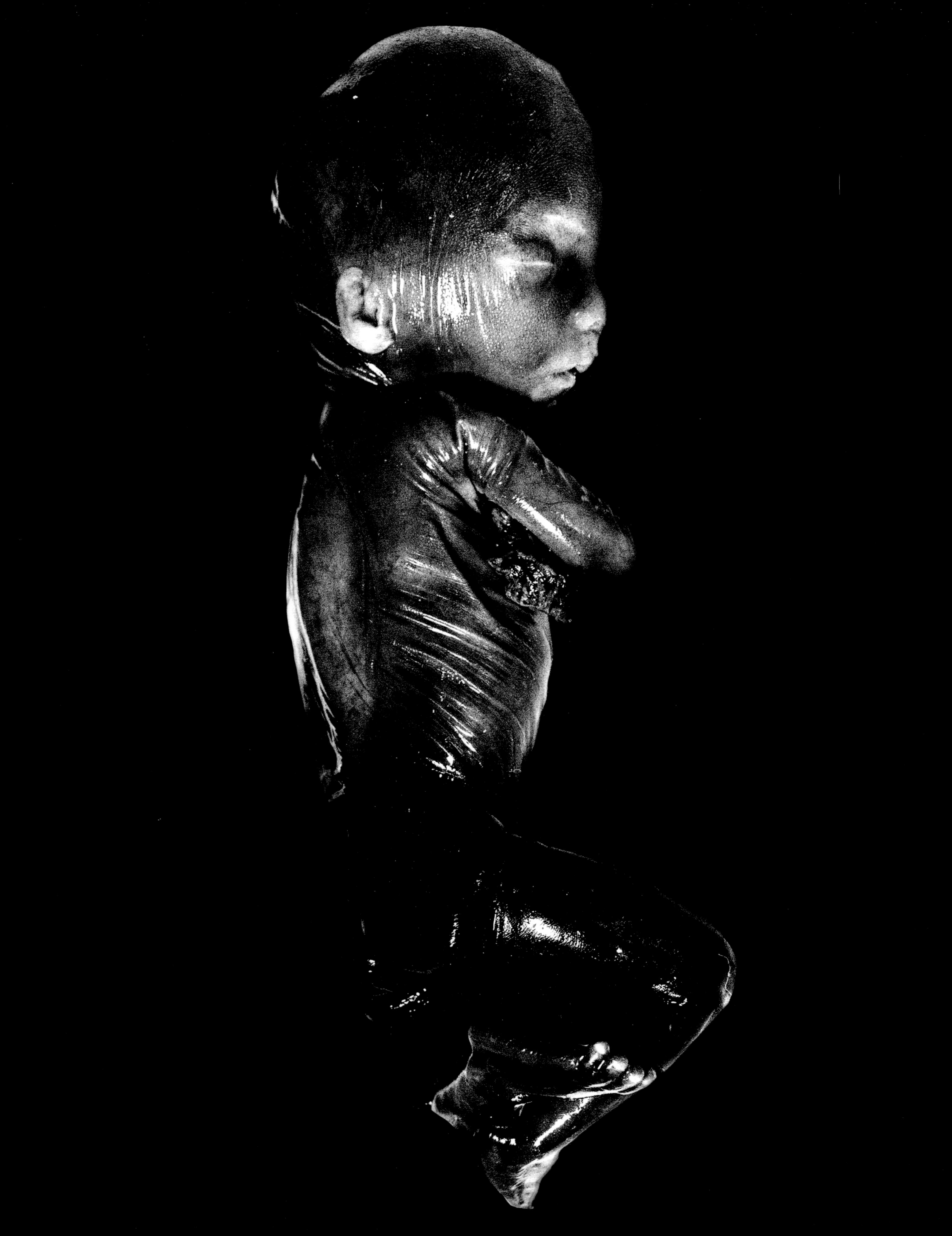

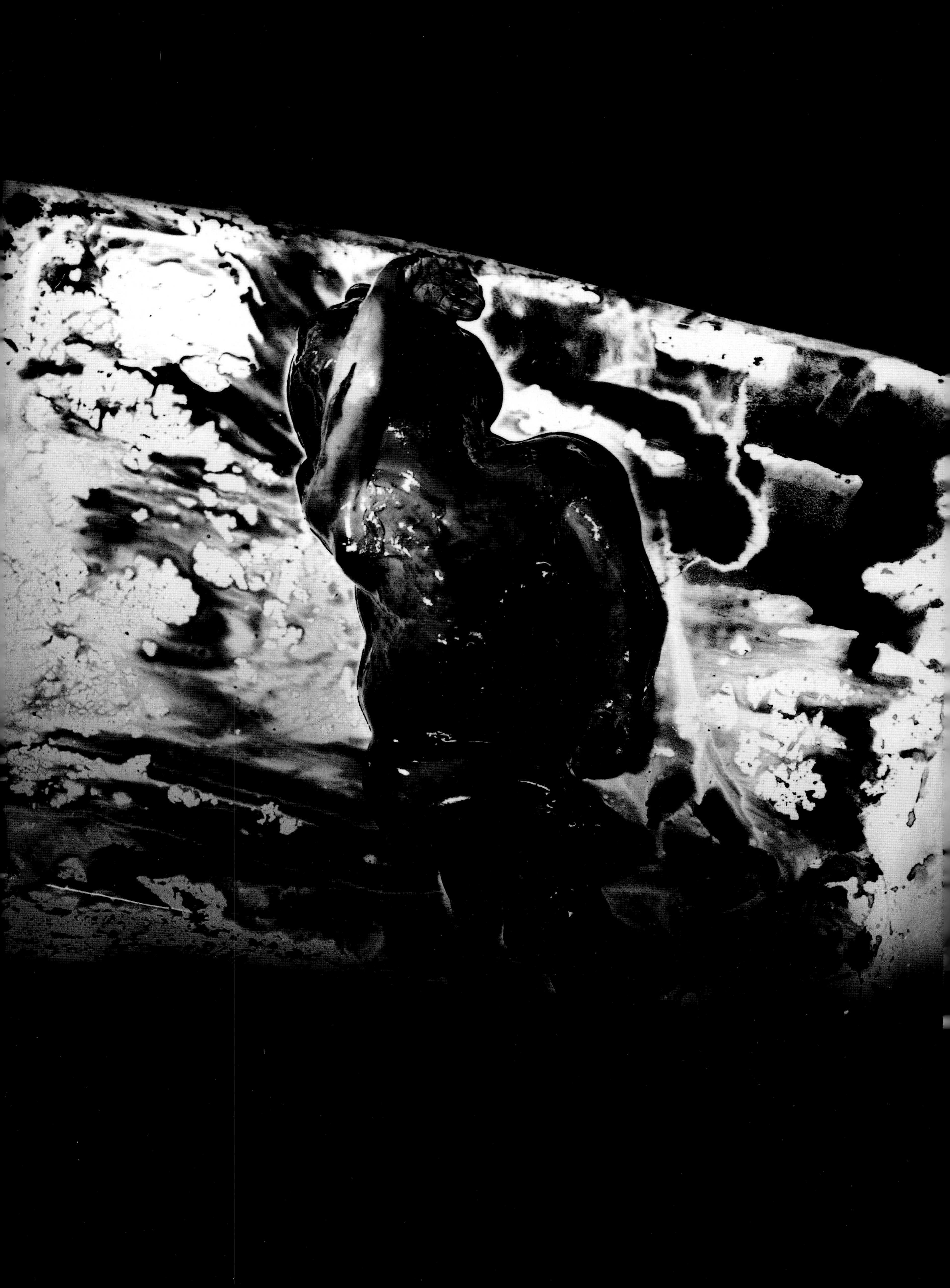

HERCULANEUM

1985–90

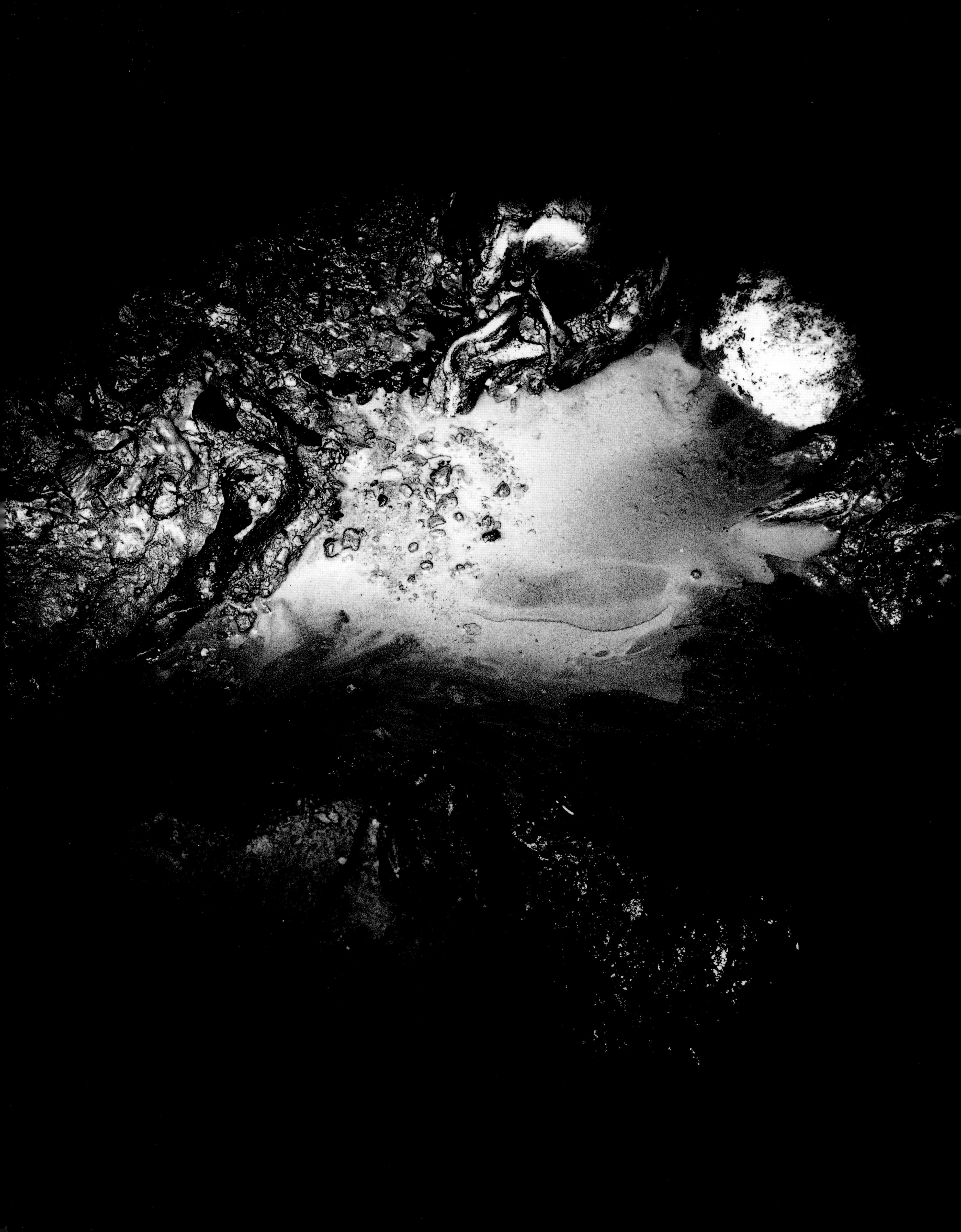

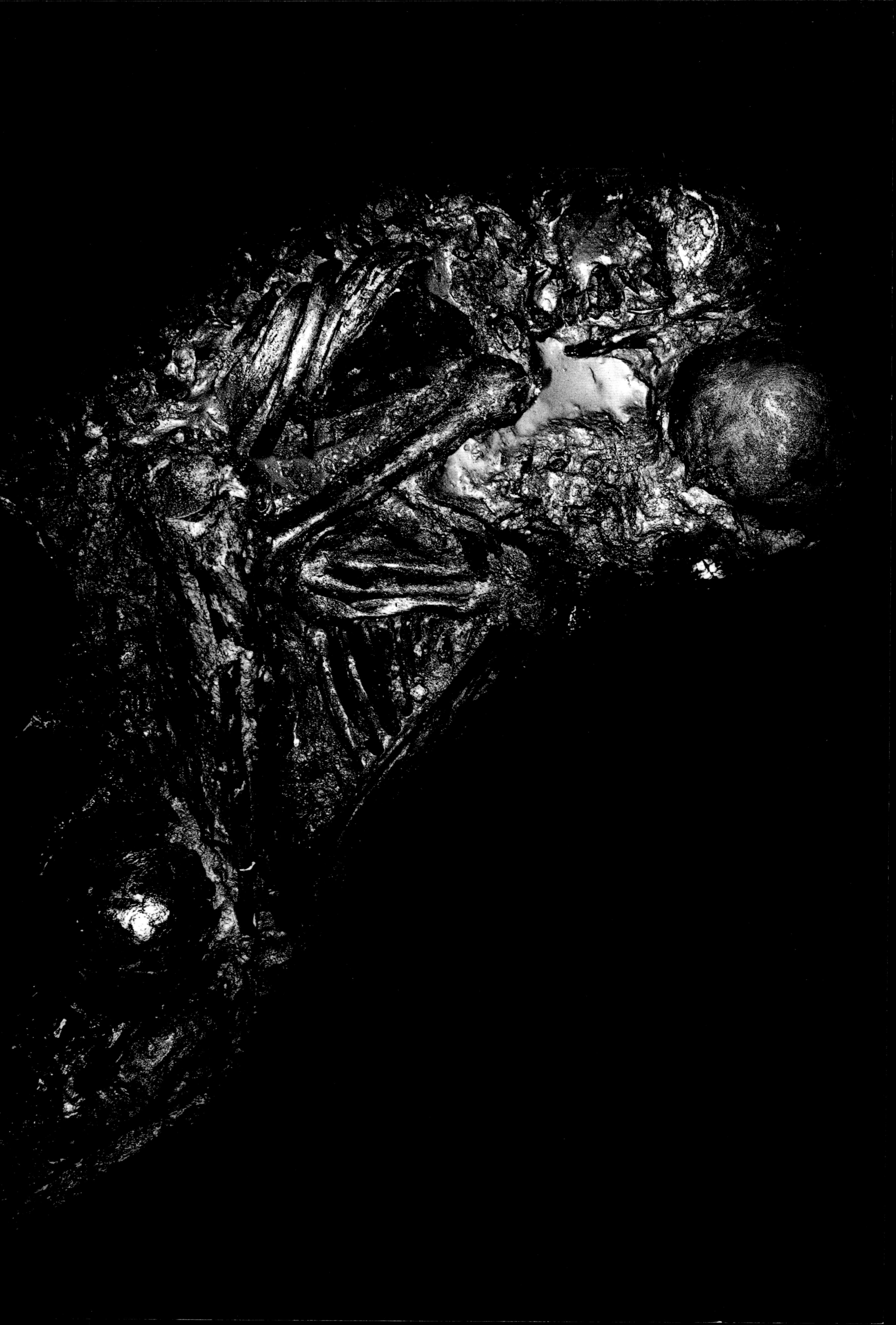

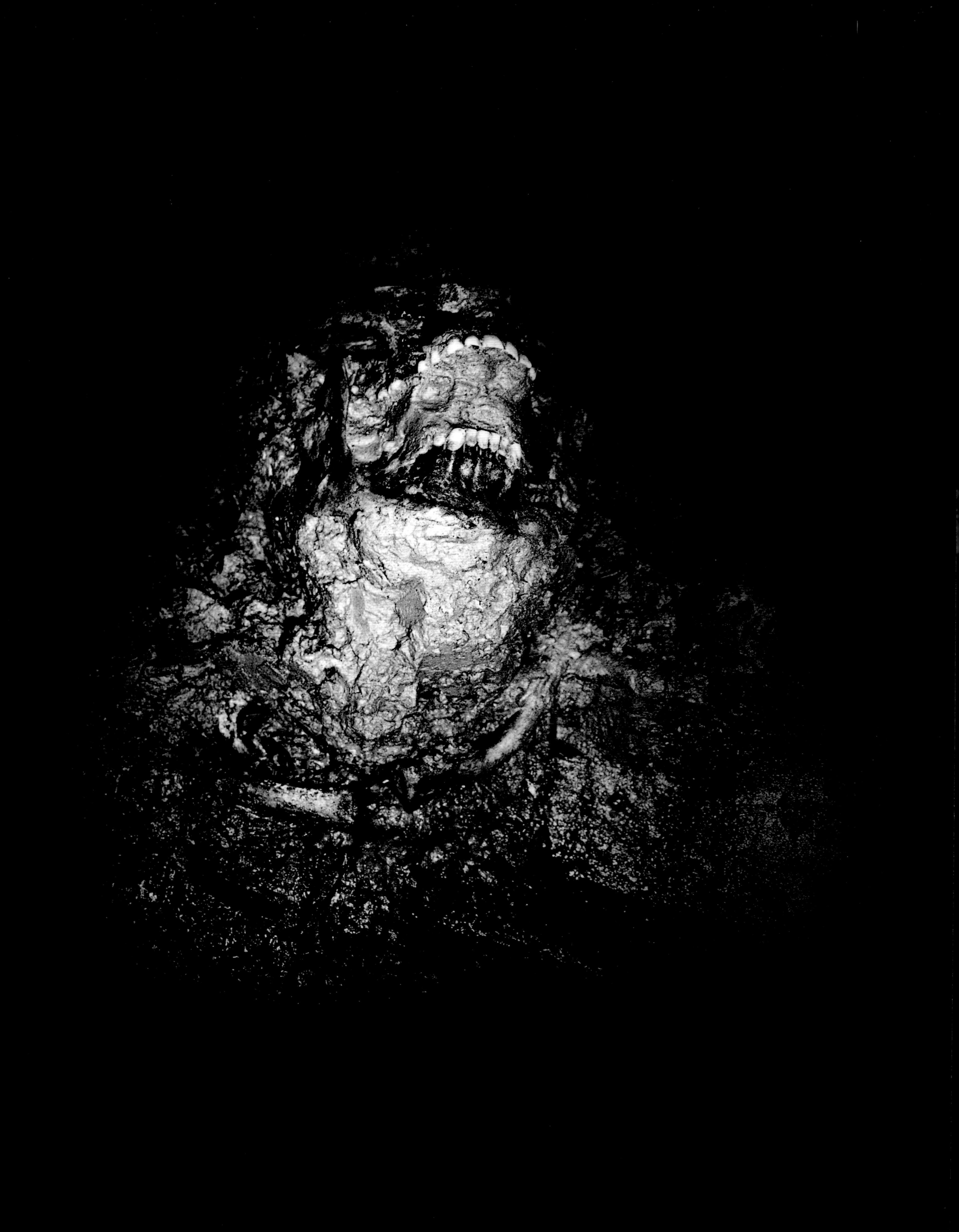

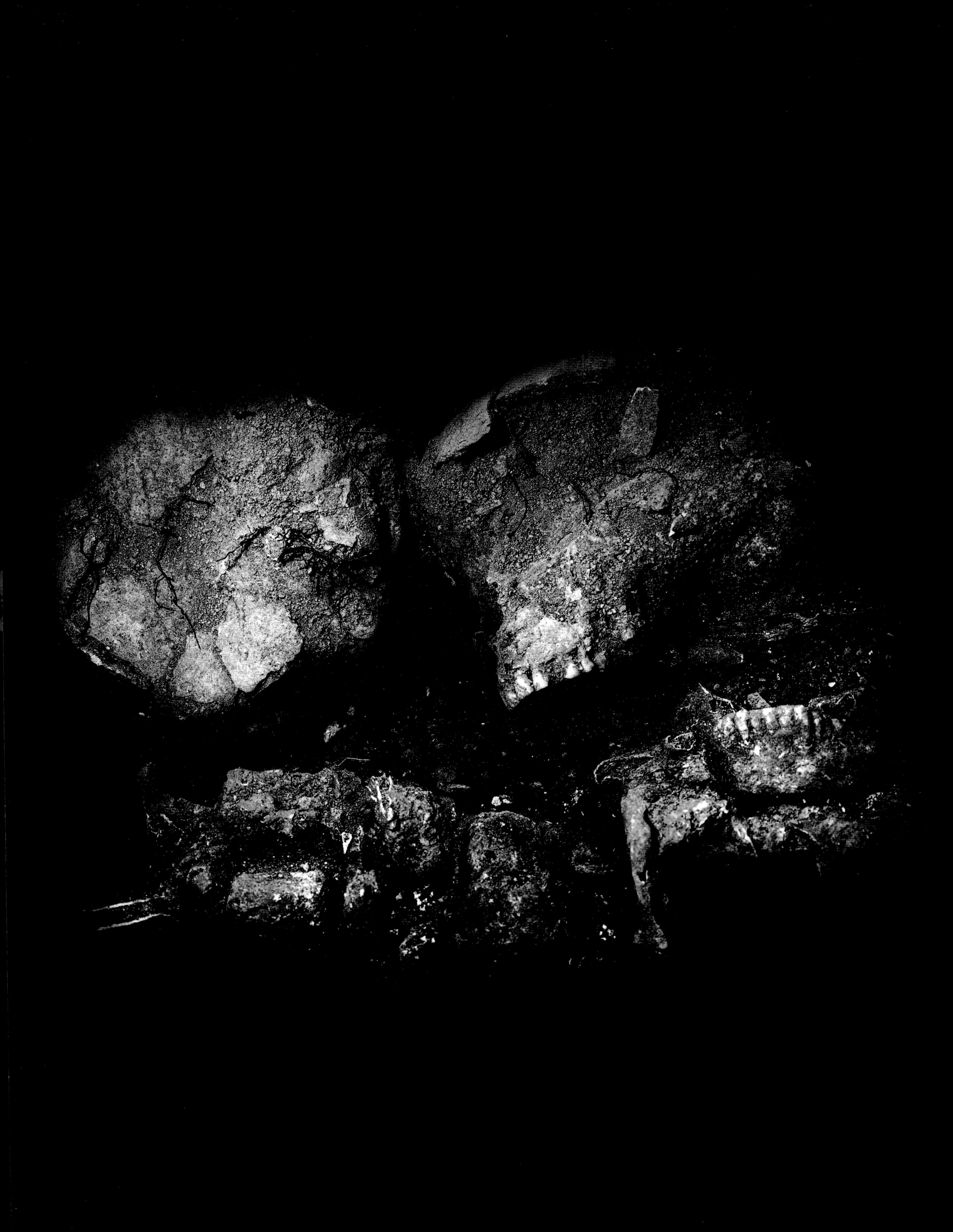

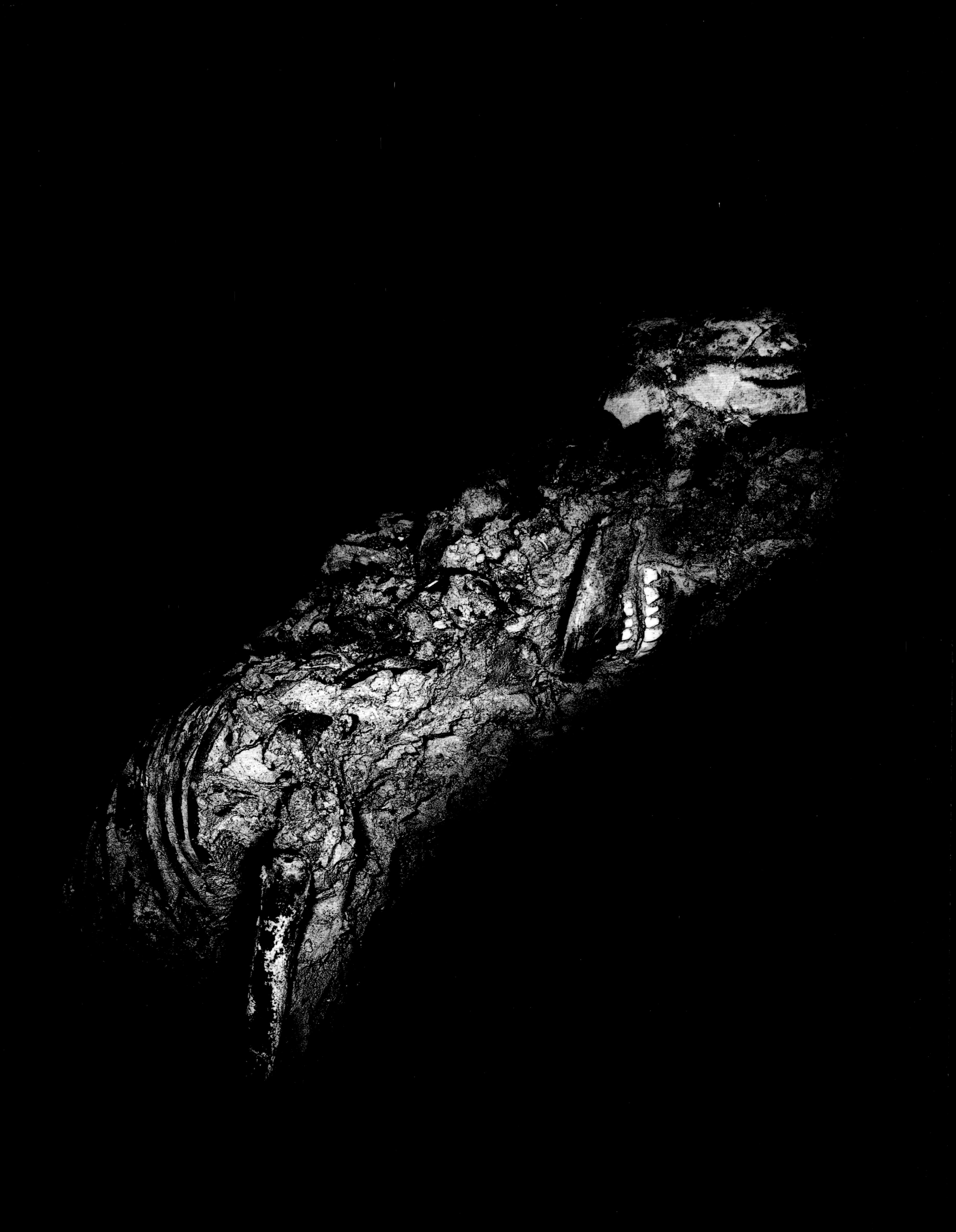

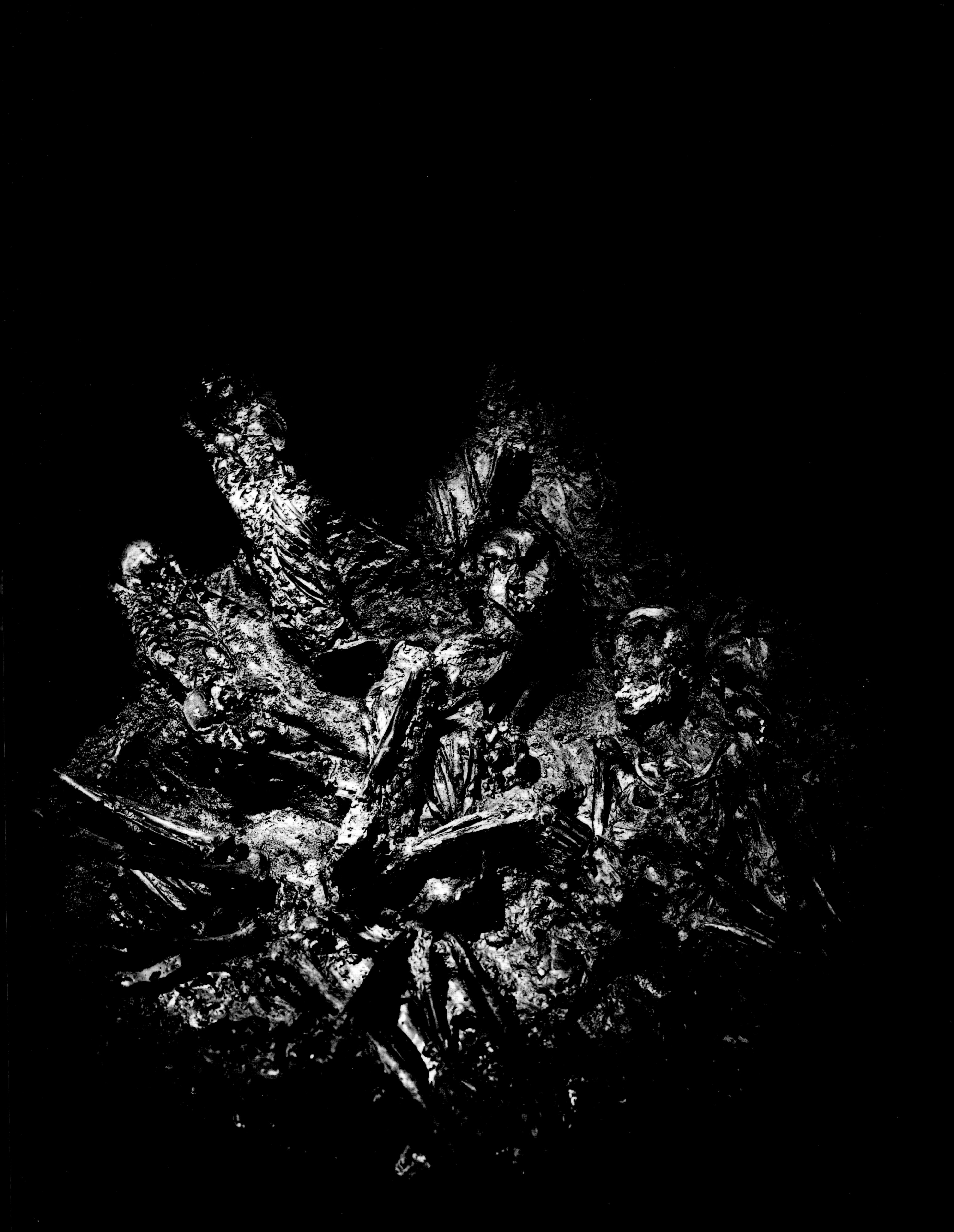

SLAUGHTERHOUSE

BOUCHERIE

SCHLACHTHOF

1985

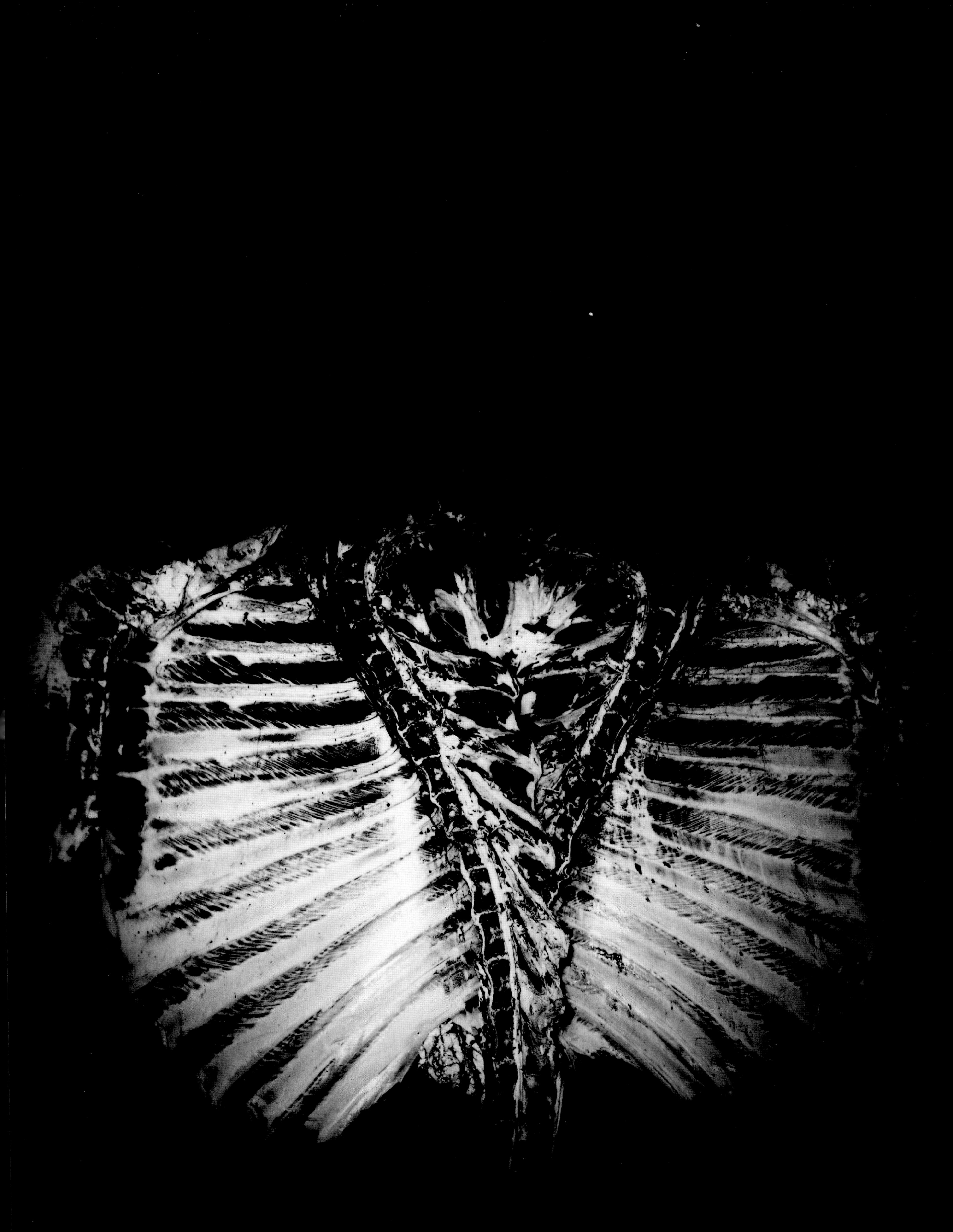

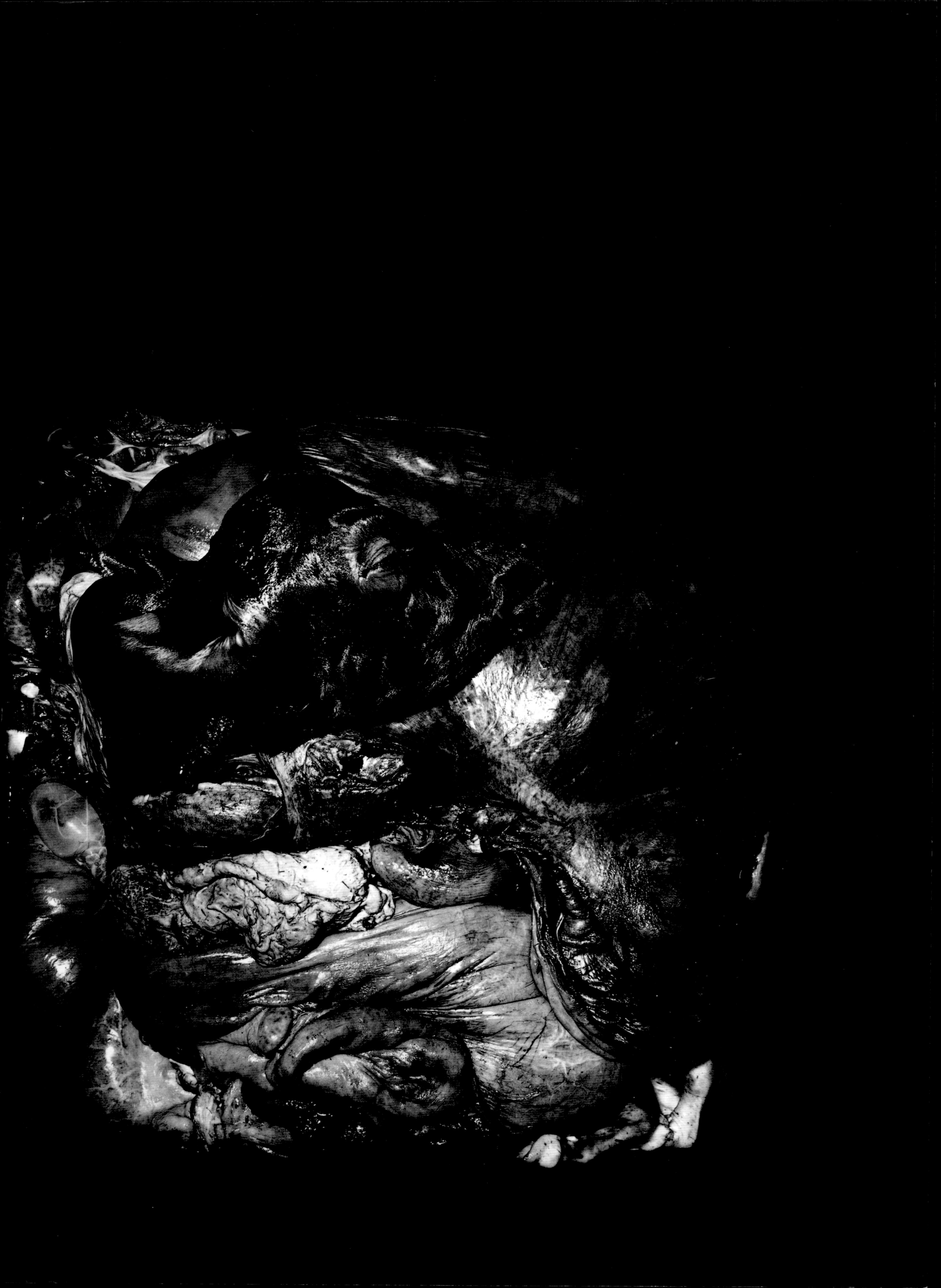

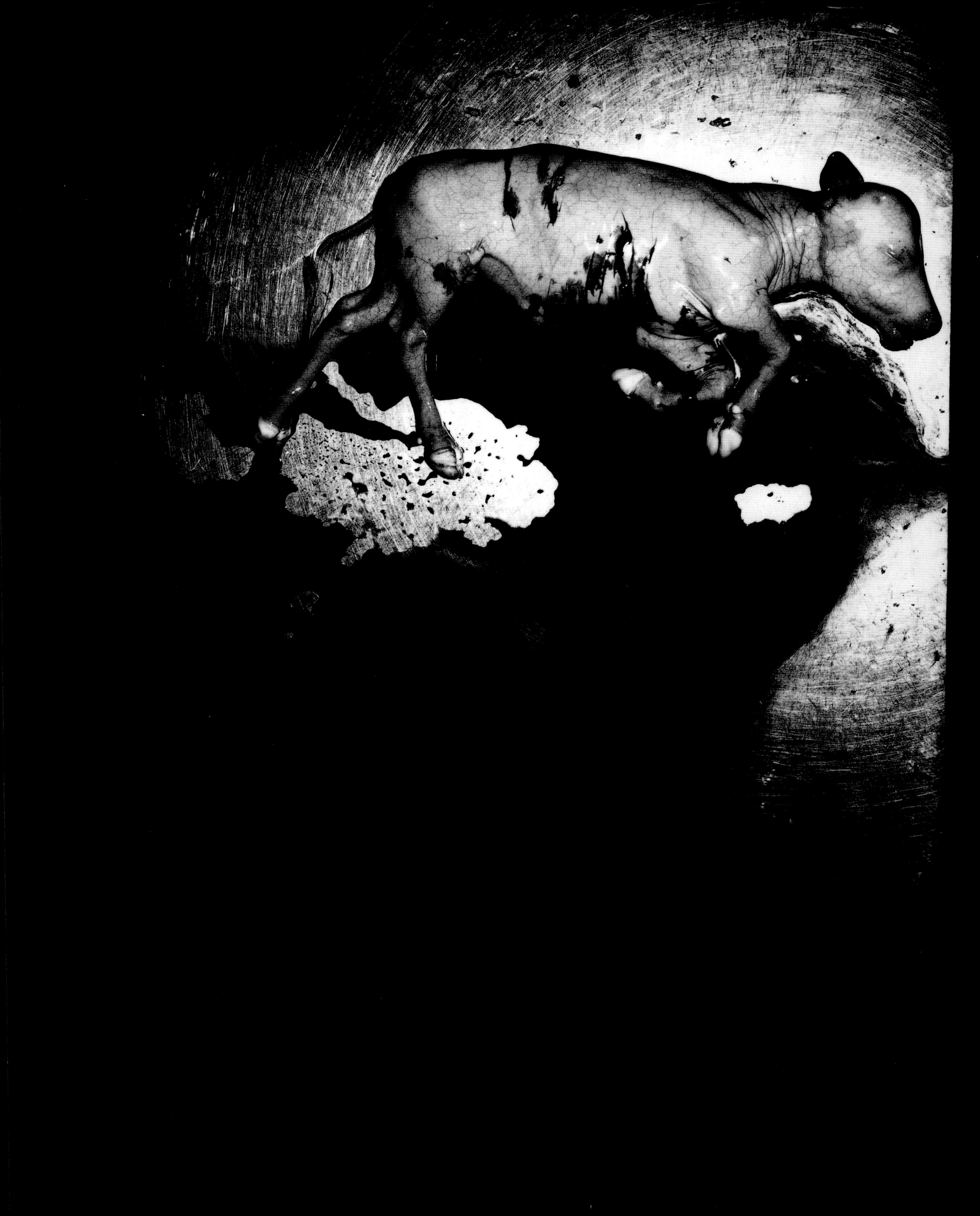

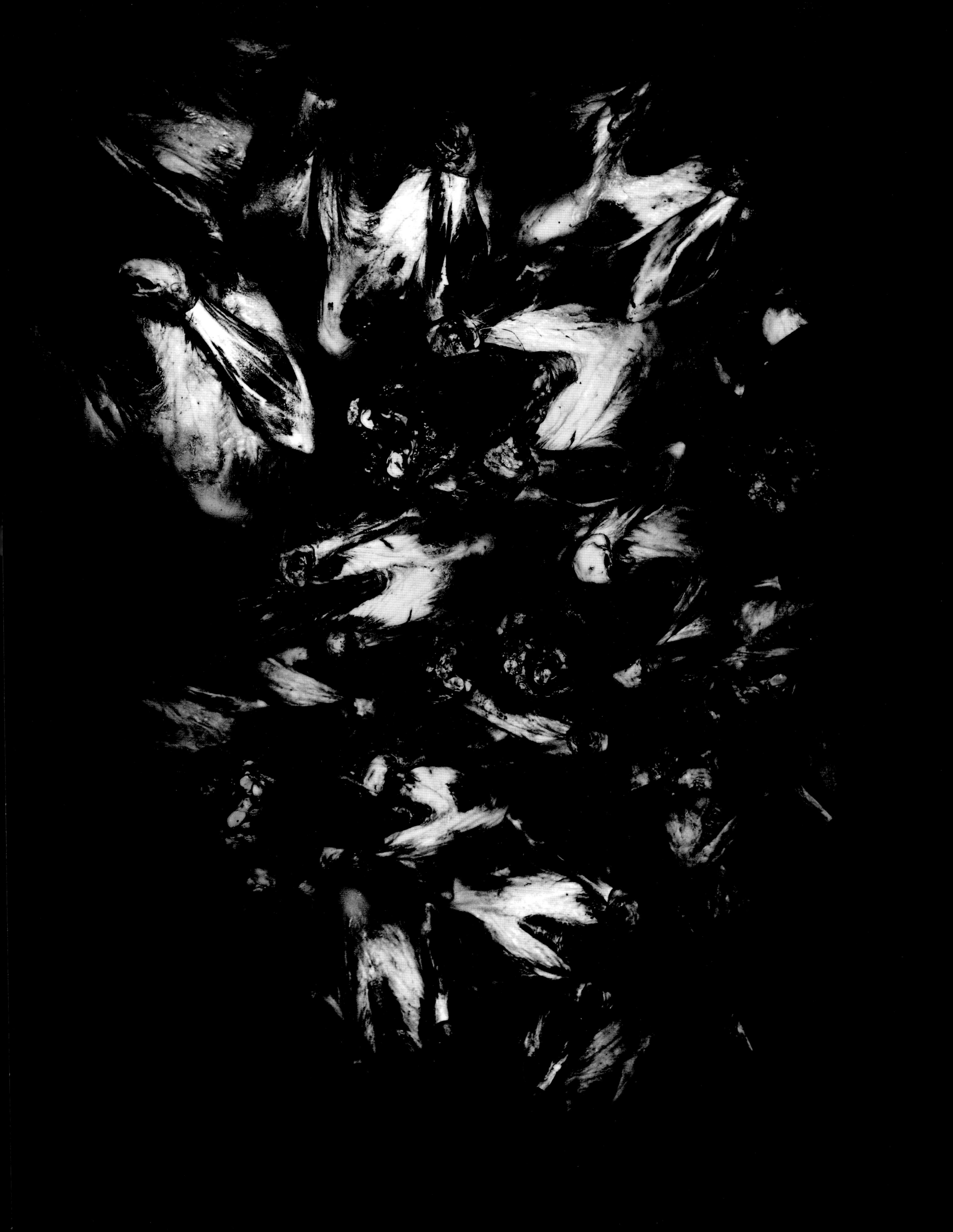

PRINT OF THE HANGED MAN

L'EMPREINTE DU PENDU

DER ABDRUCK DES ERHÄNGTEN

1987

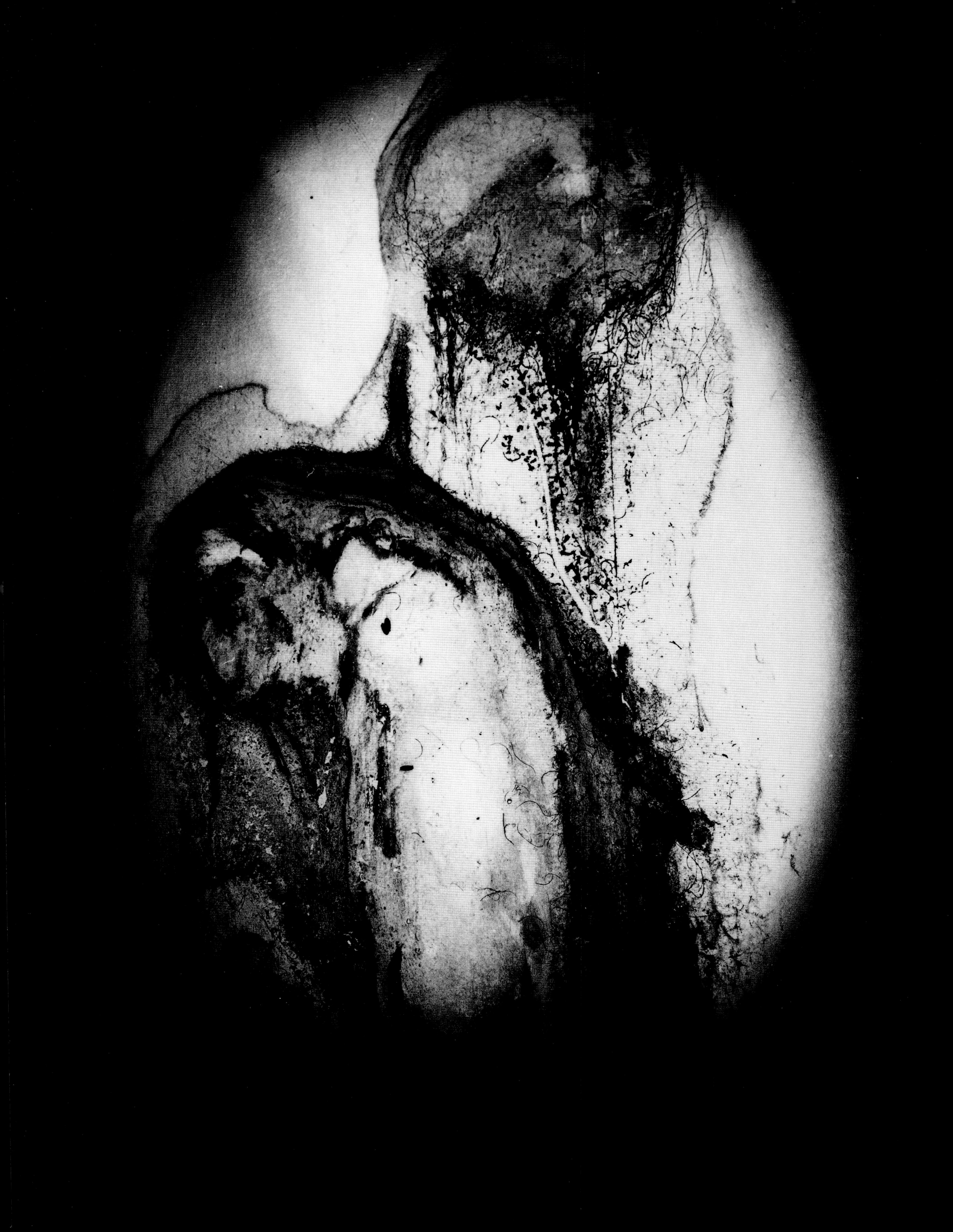

FÈS

1989

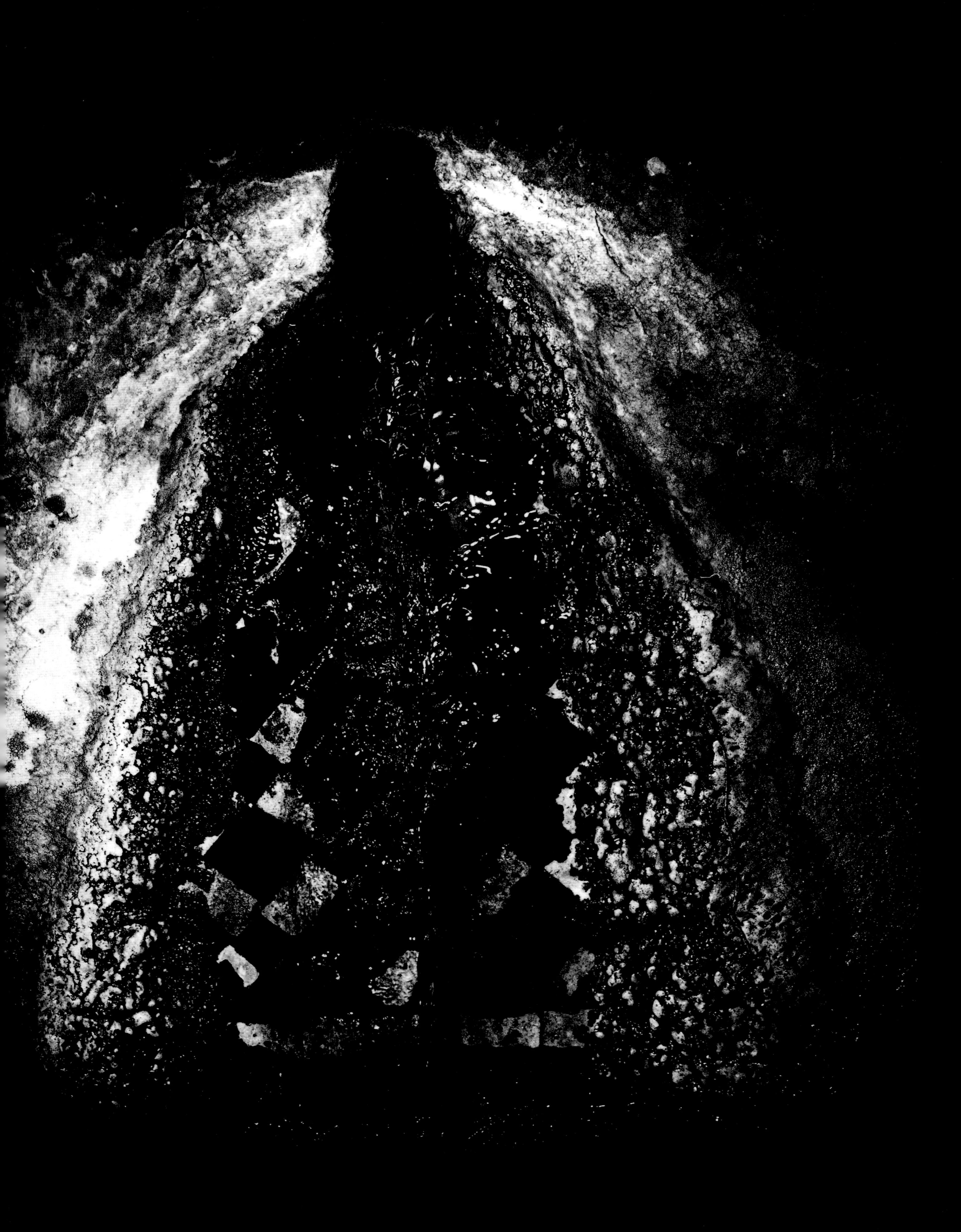

بسم الله الرحمن الرحيم
يأيتها النفس المطمئنة
ارجعي الى ربك راضية
فادخلي في عبادي
الله روح الشريف

LASCAUX

1990

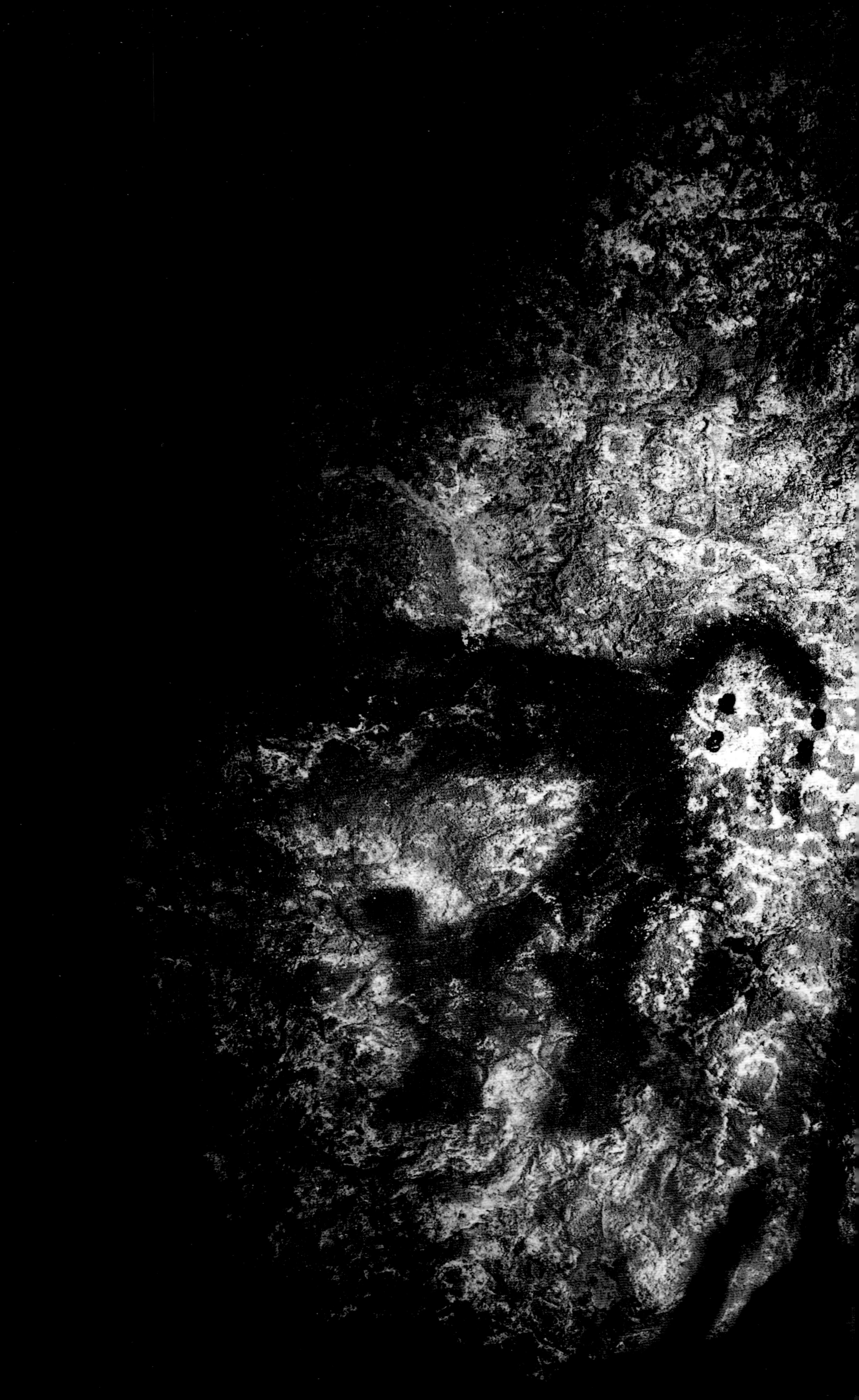

PALEONTOLOGICAL TRACES
VESTIGES PALÉONTOLOGIQUES
PALÄONTOLOGISCHE SPUREN

1991

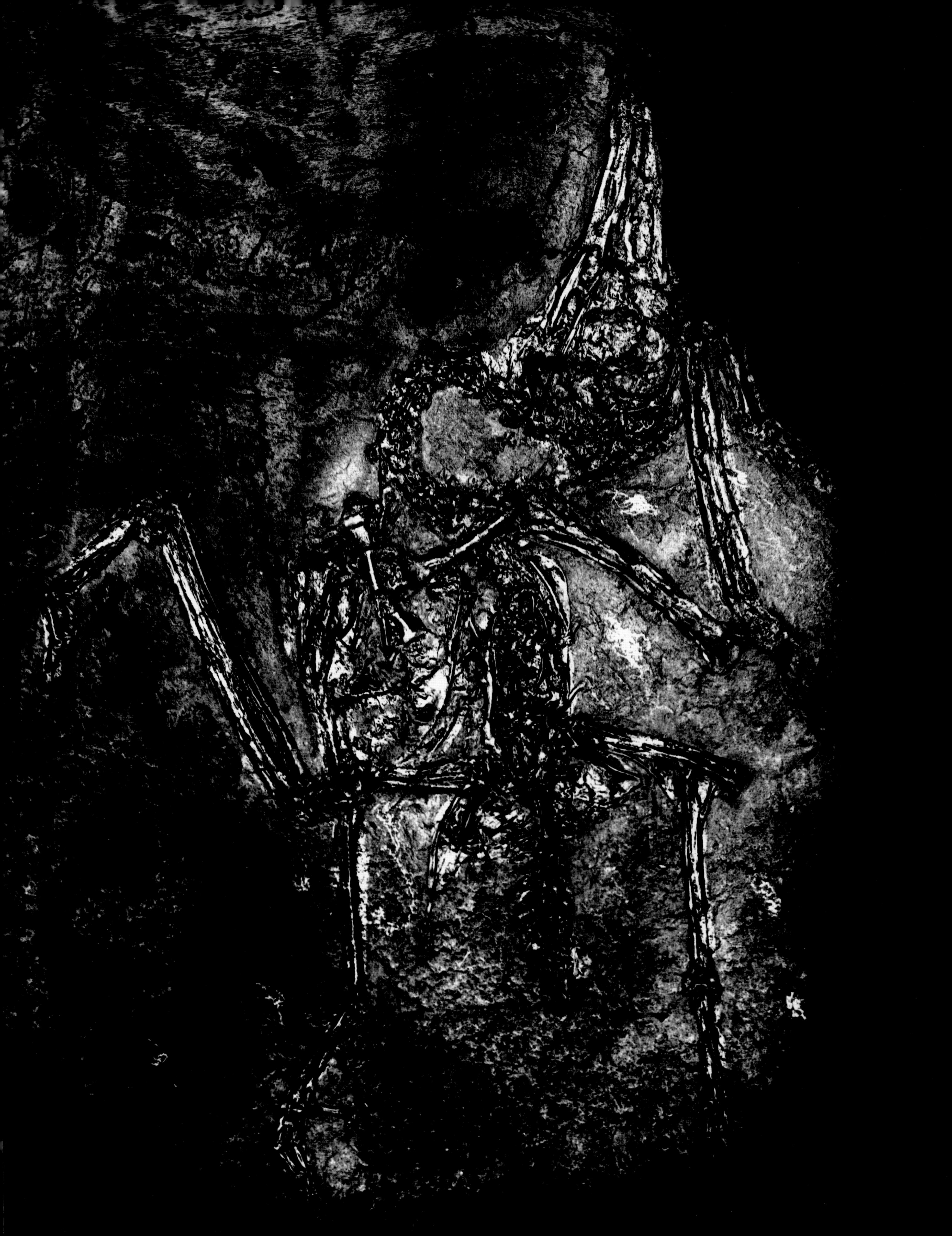

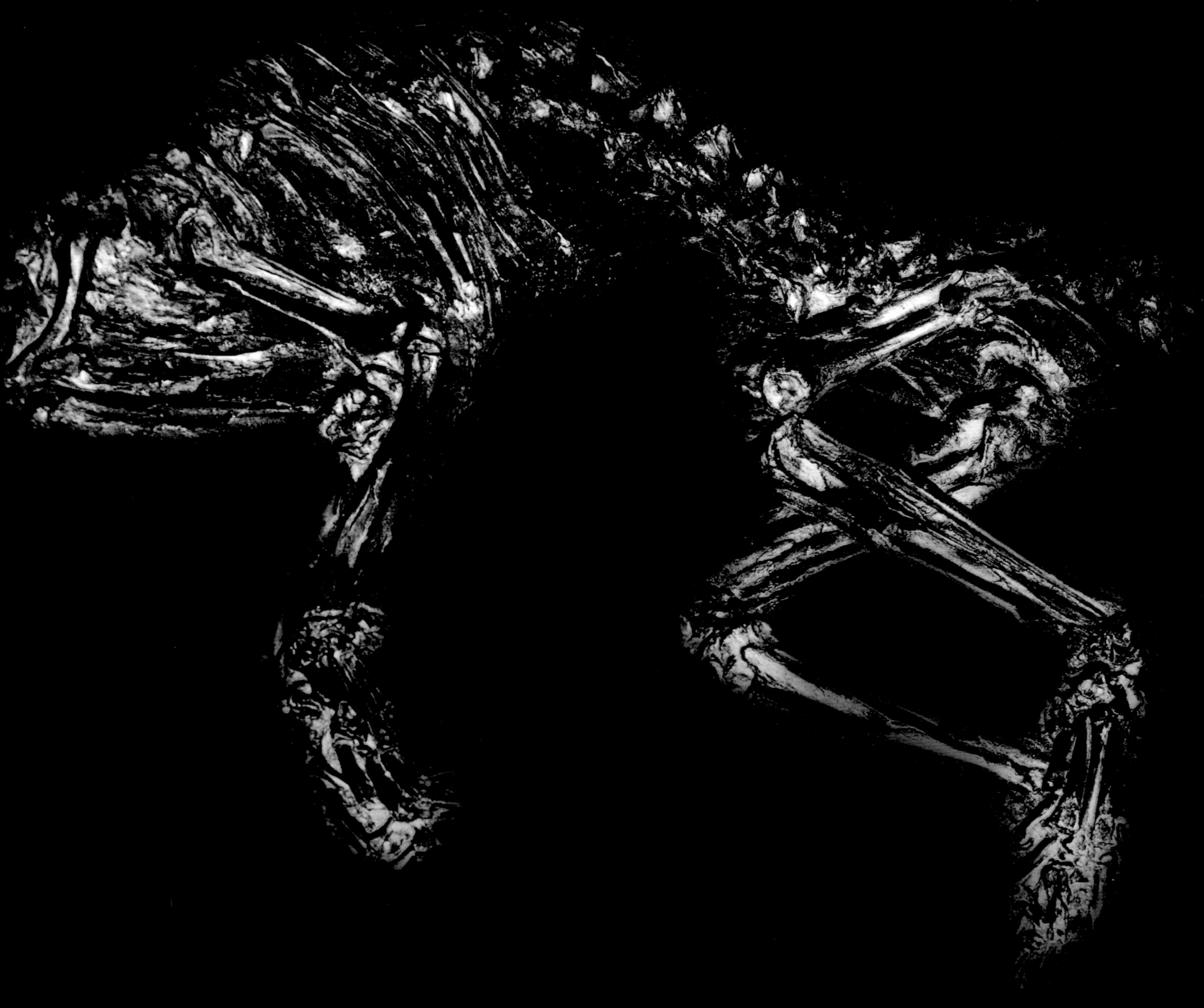

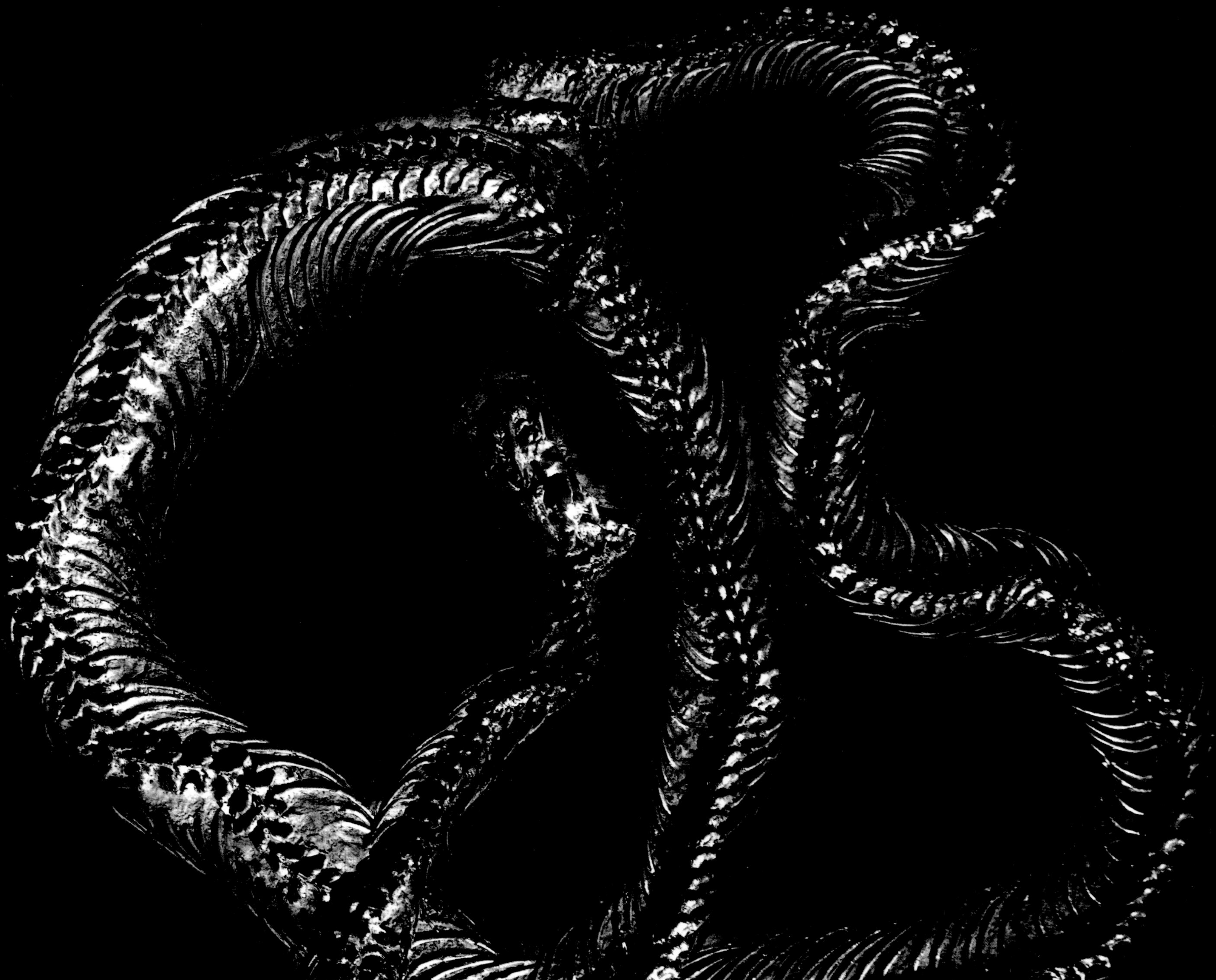

AUSCHWITZ

1992

37
Transpor

HEDVIG
GEB 1896
HERM AN
474
725

THE MAN IN THE ICE

L'HOMME DES GLACES

DER MENSCH AUS DEM EIS

1992

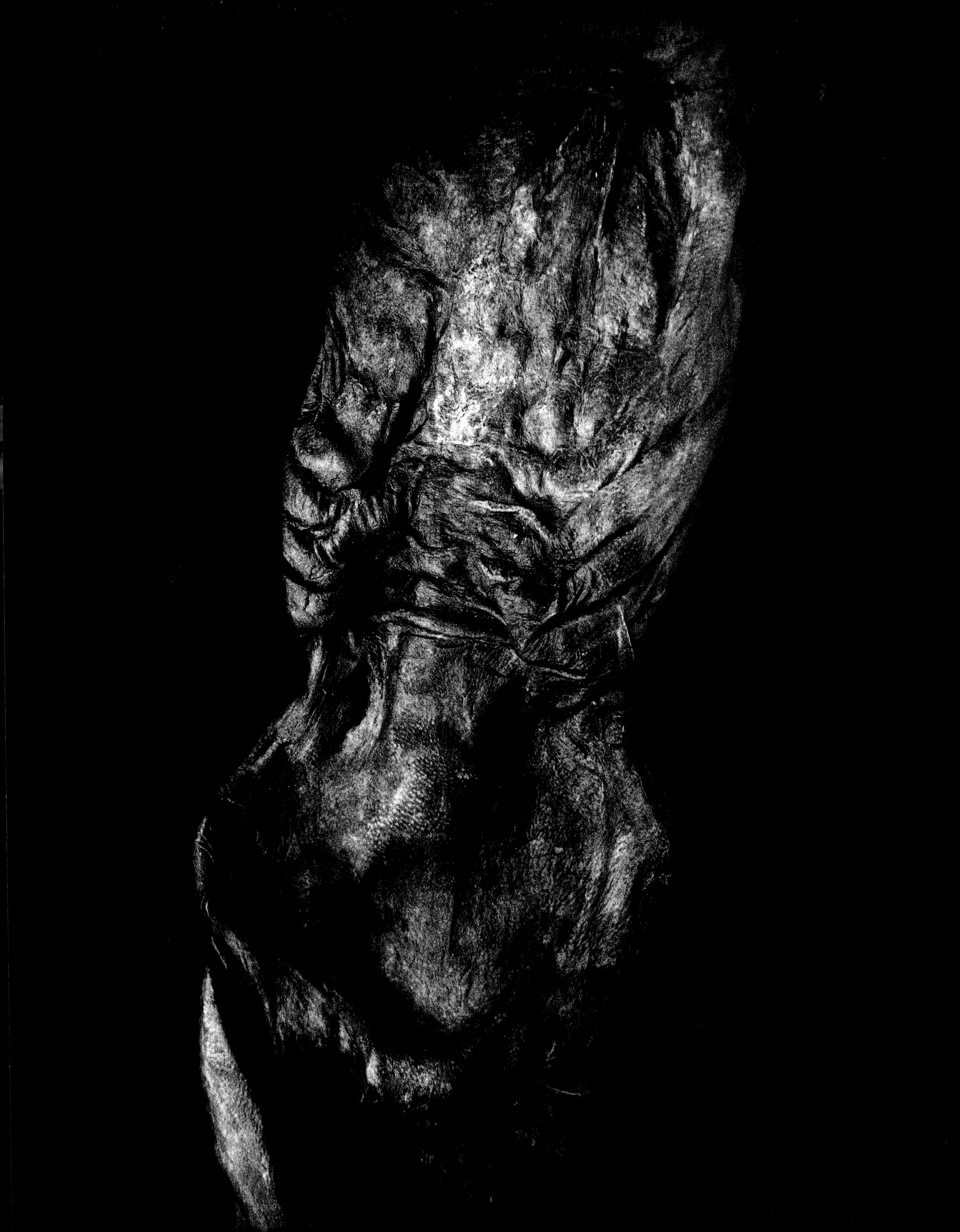

SQUID AND FISH

POULPE ET POISSONS

TINTENFISCH UND FISCHE

1992–93

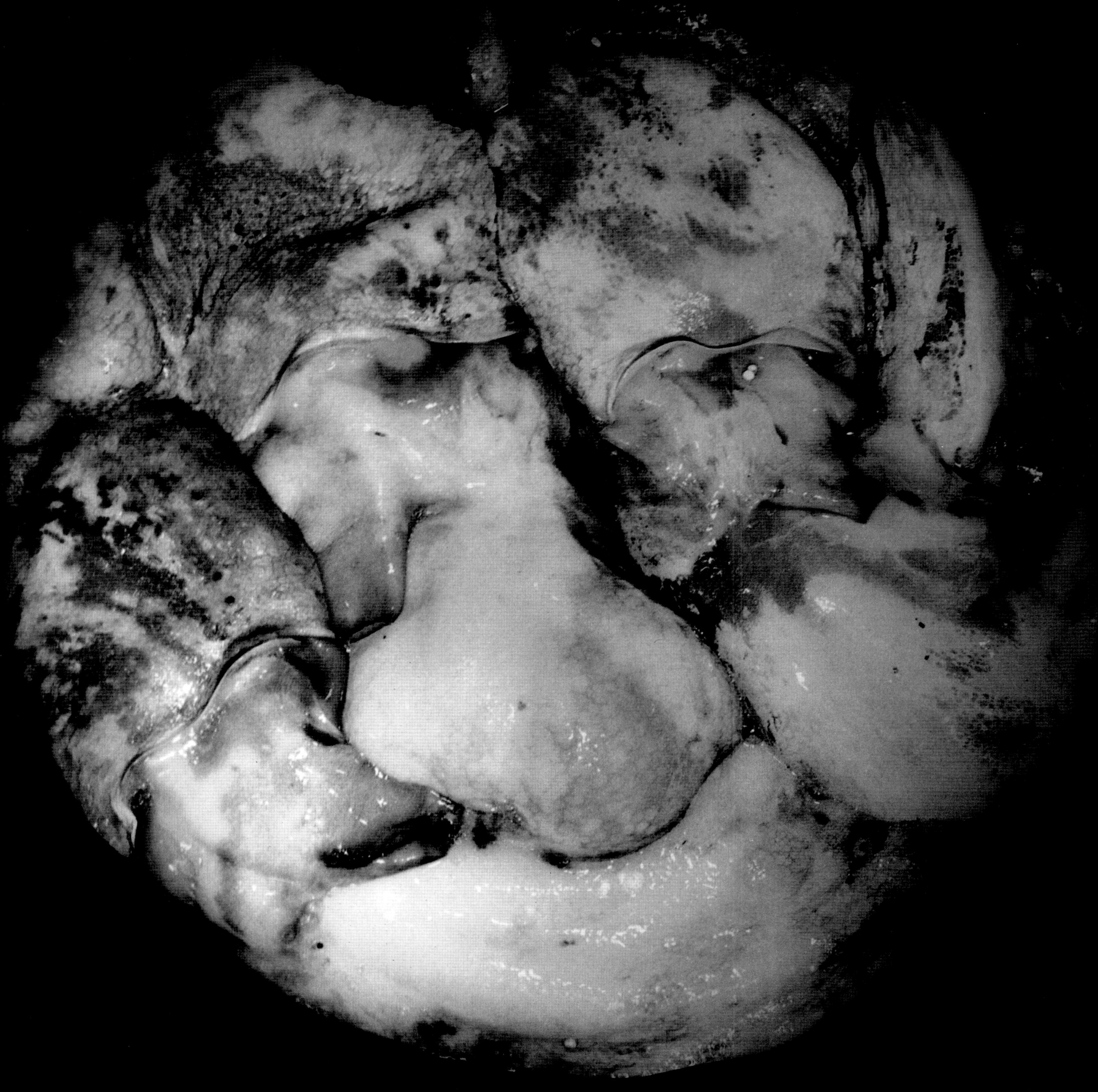

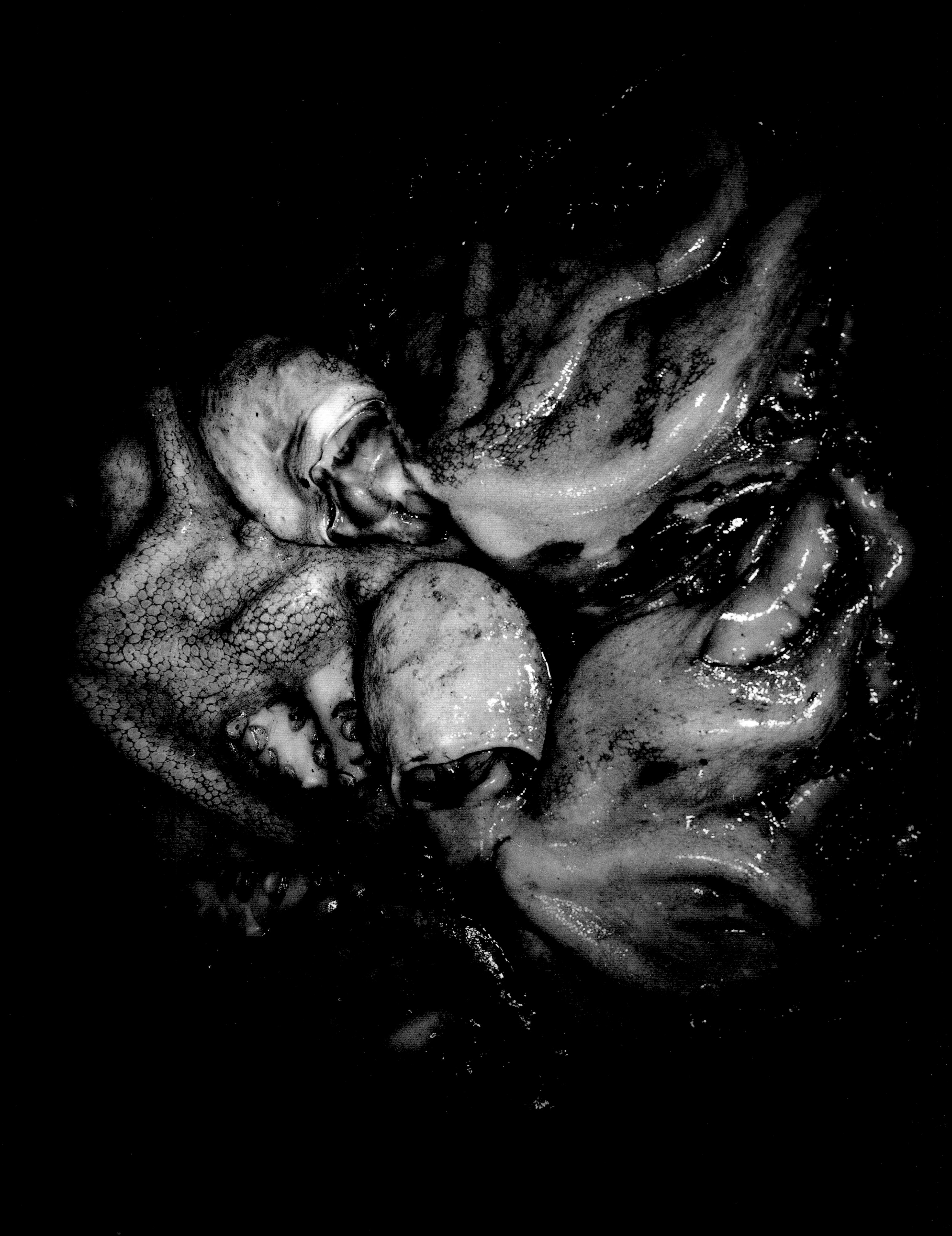

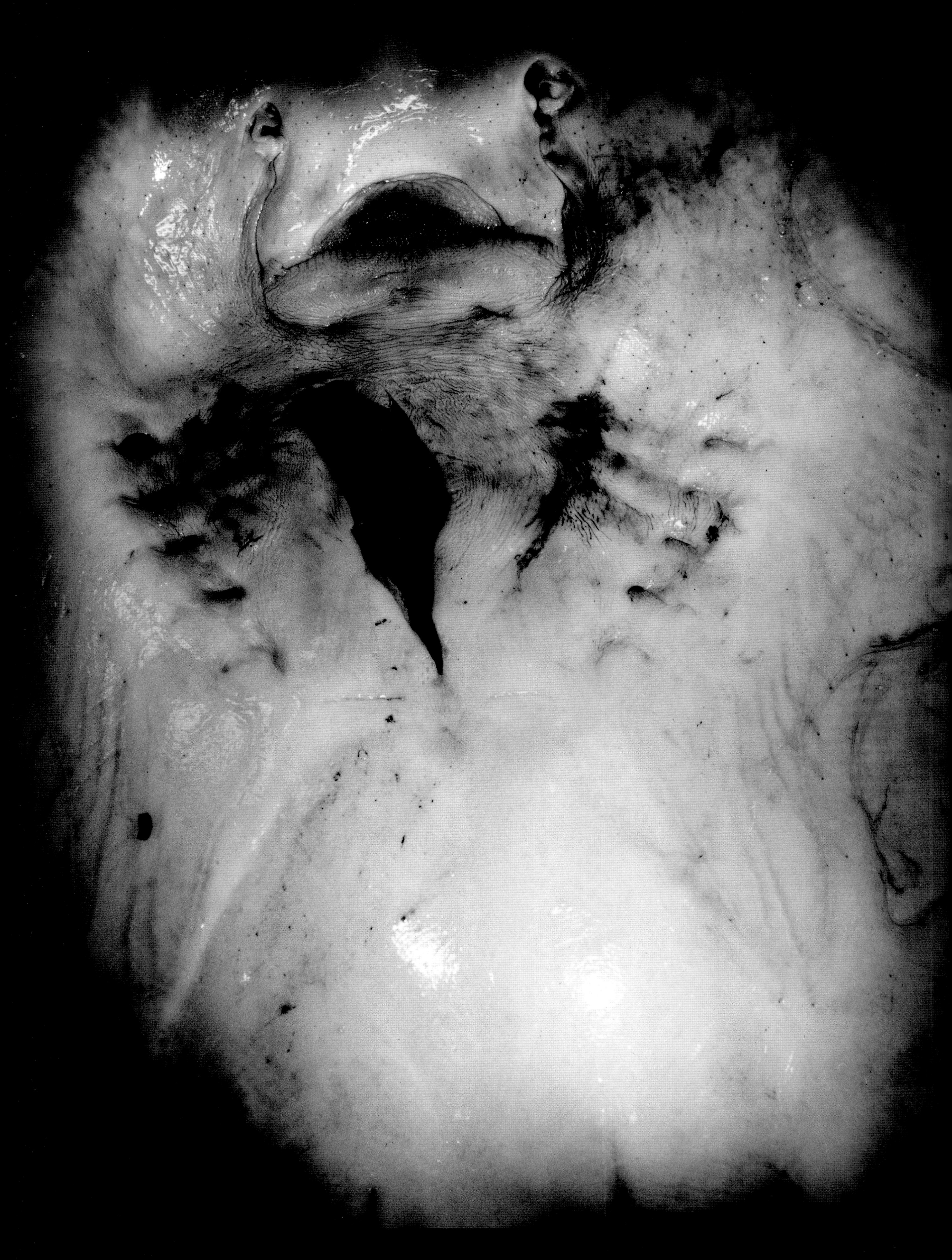

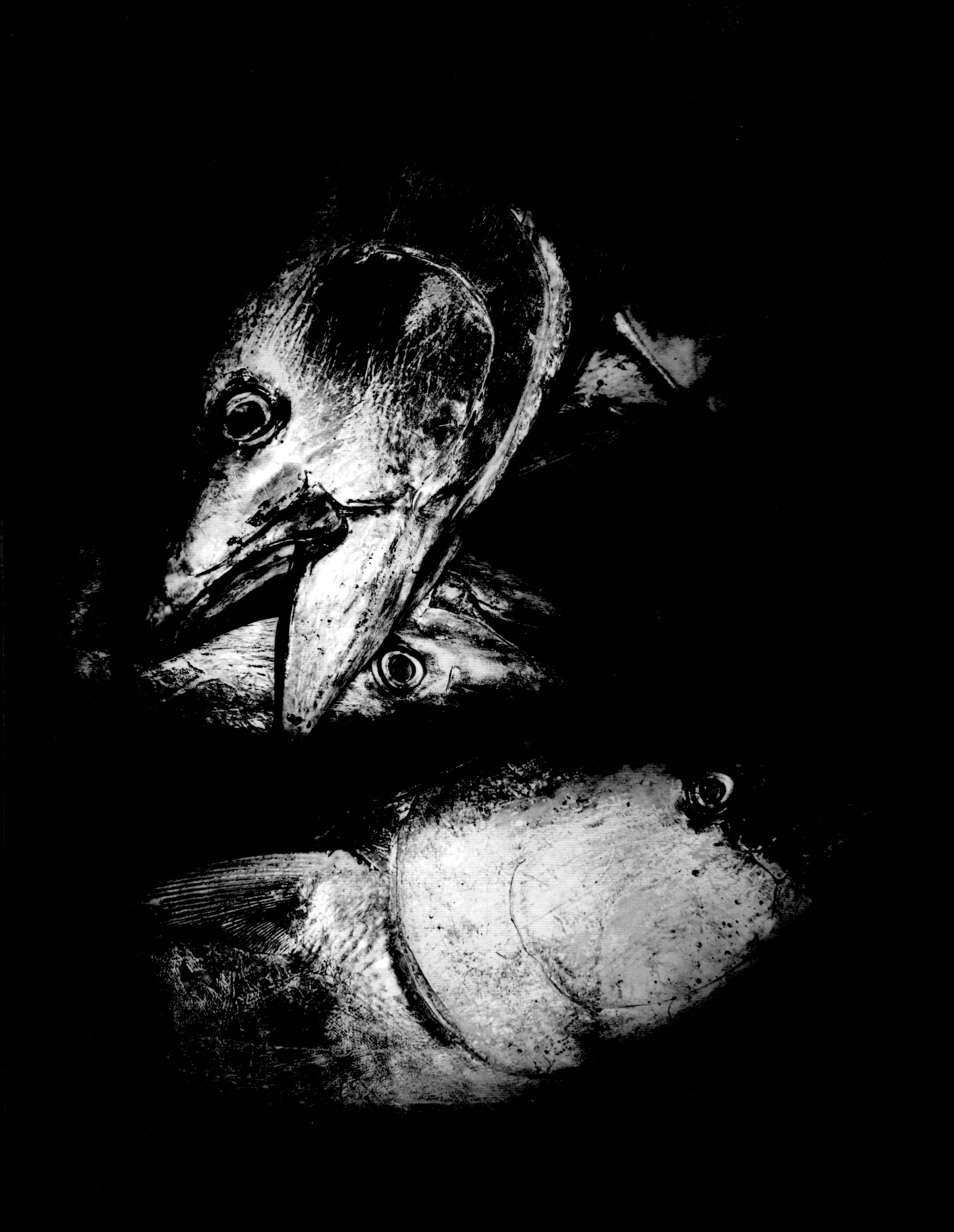

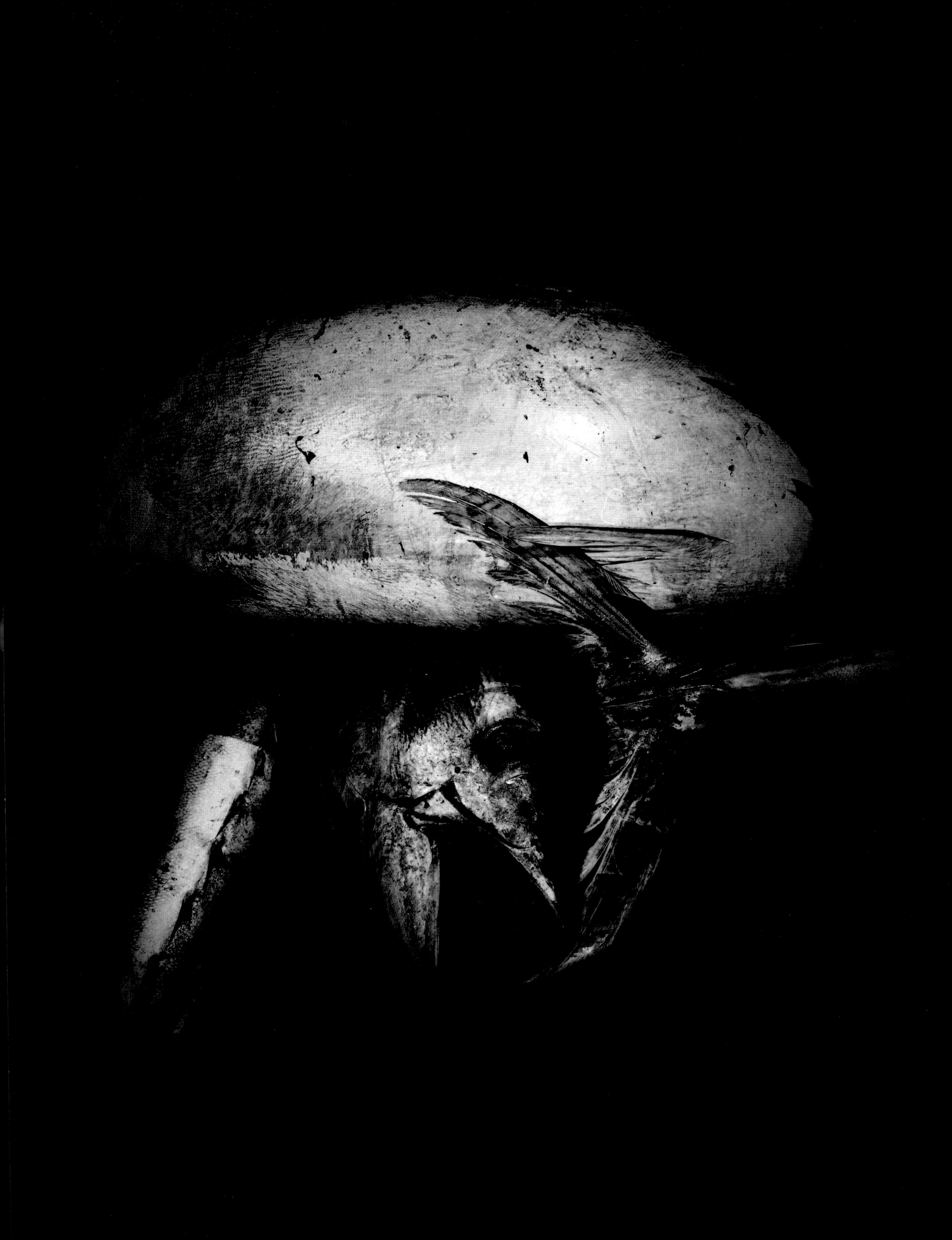

TRANCE

TRANSE

TRANCE

1993–95

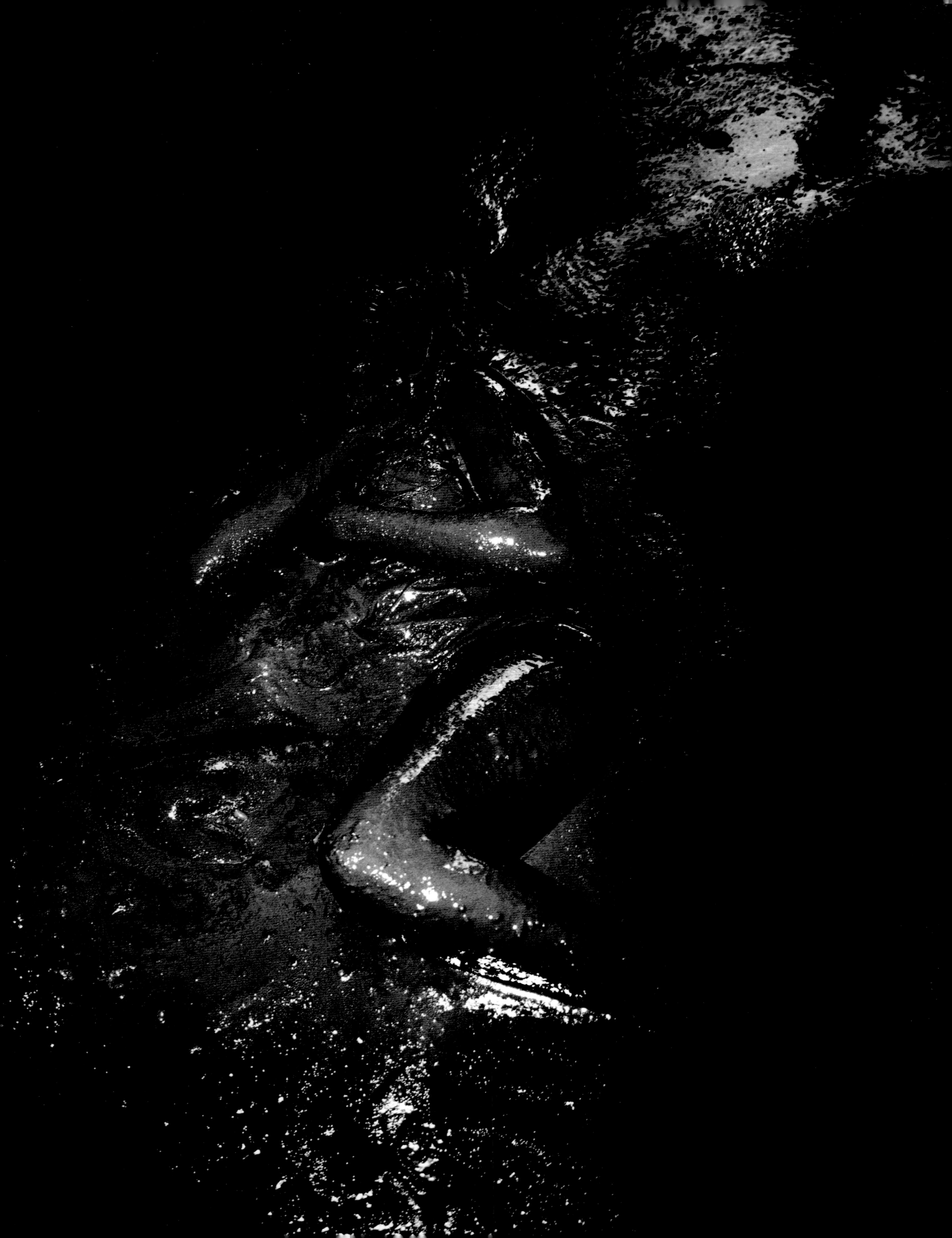

L'ALHAMBRA

1995

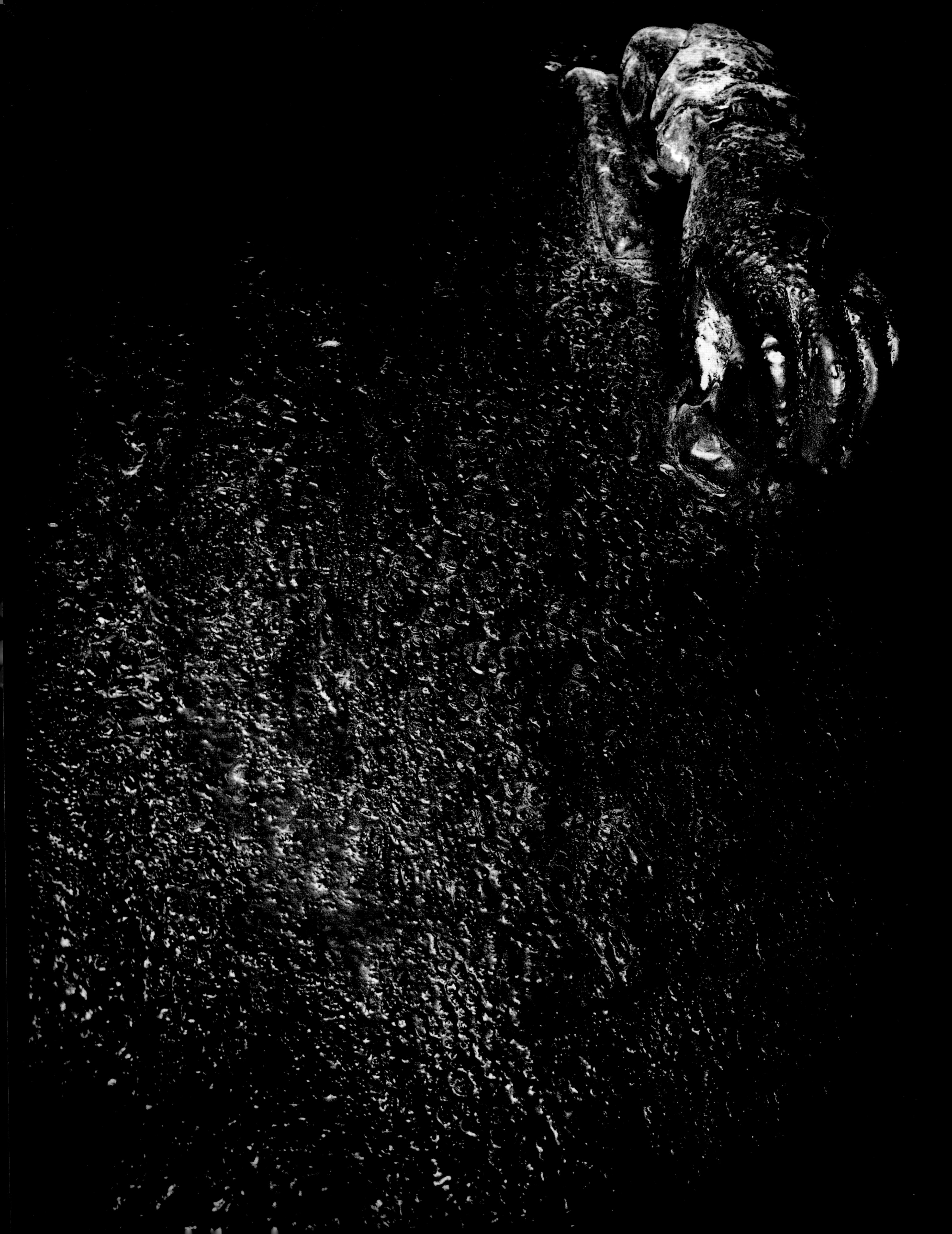

AY ! MI TORO !

1996

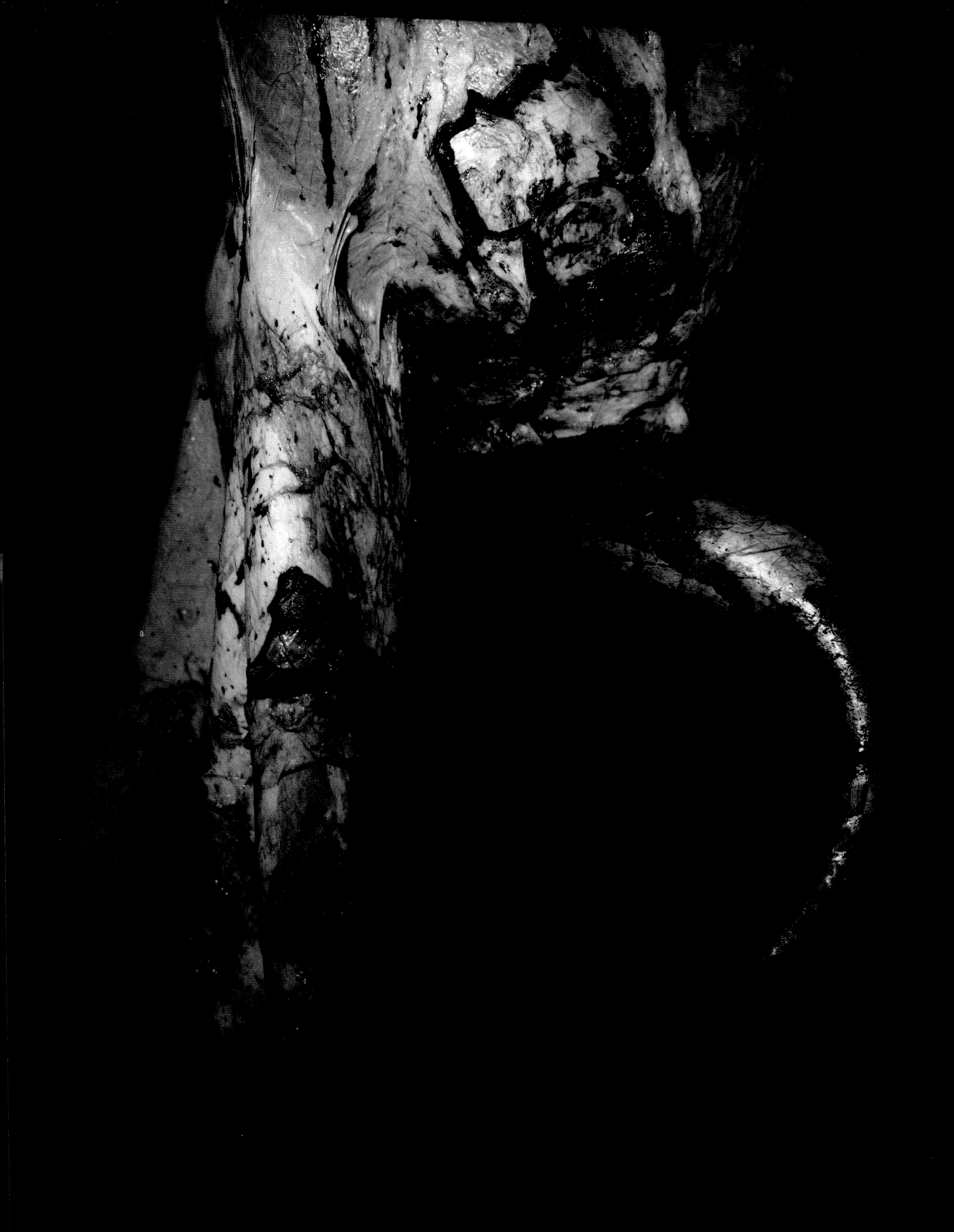

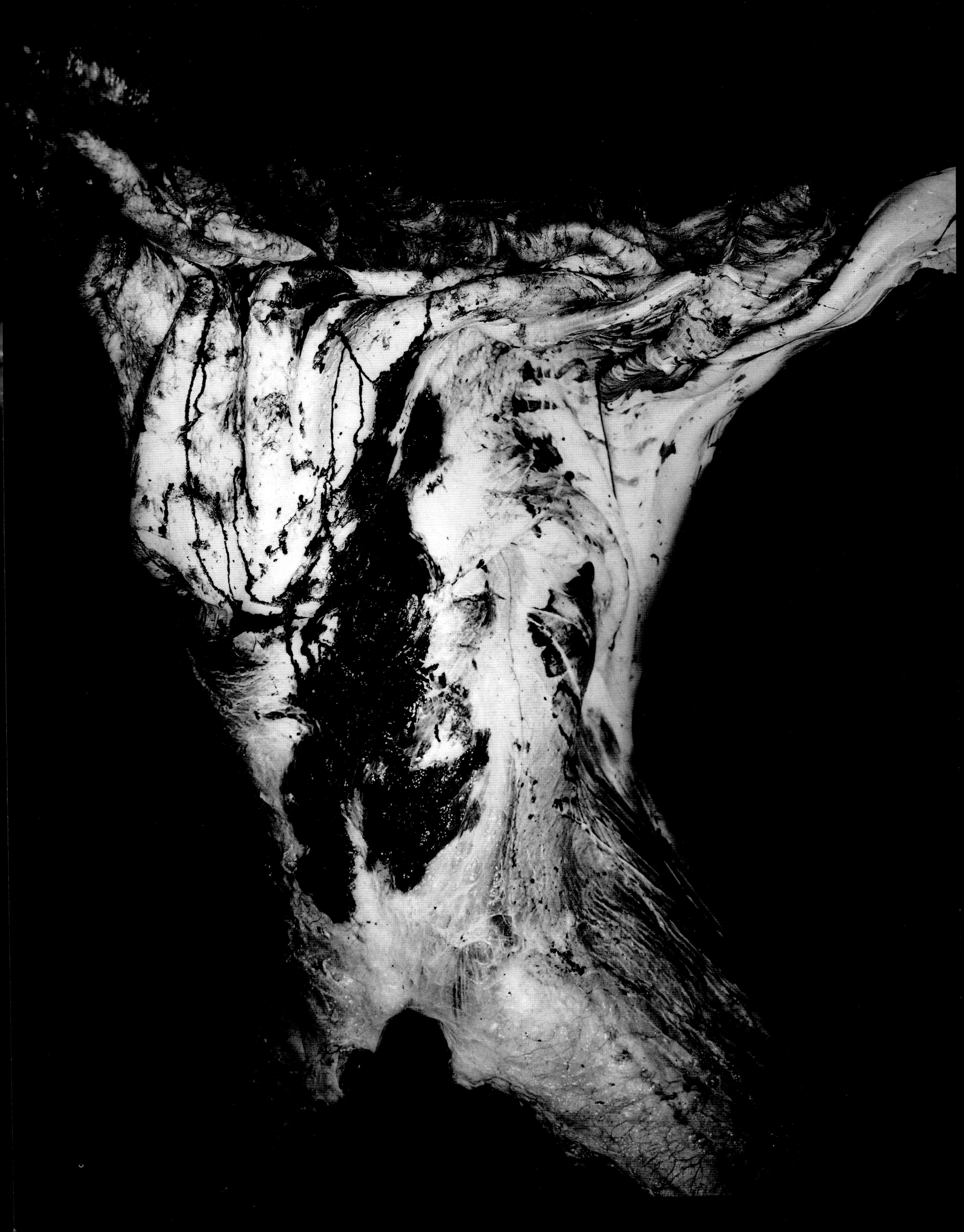

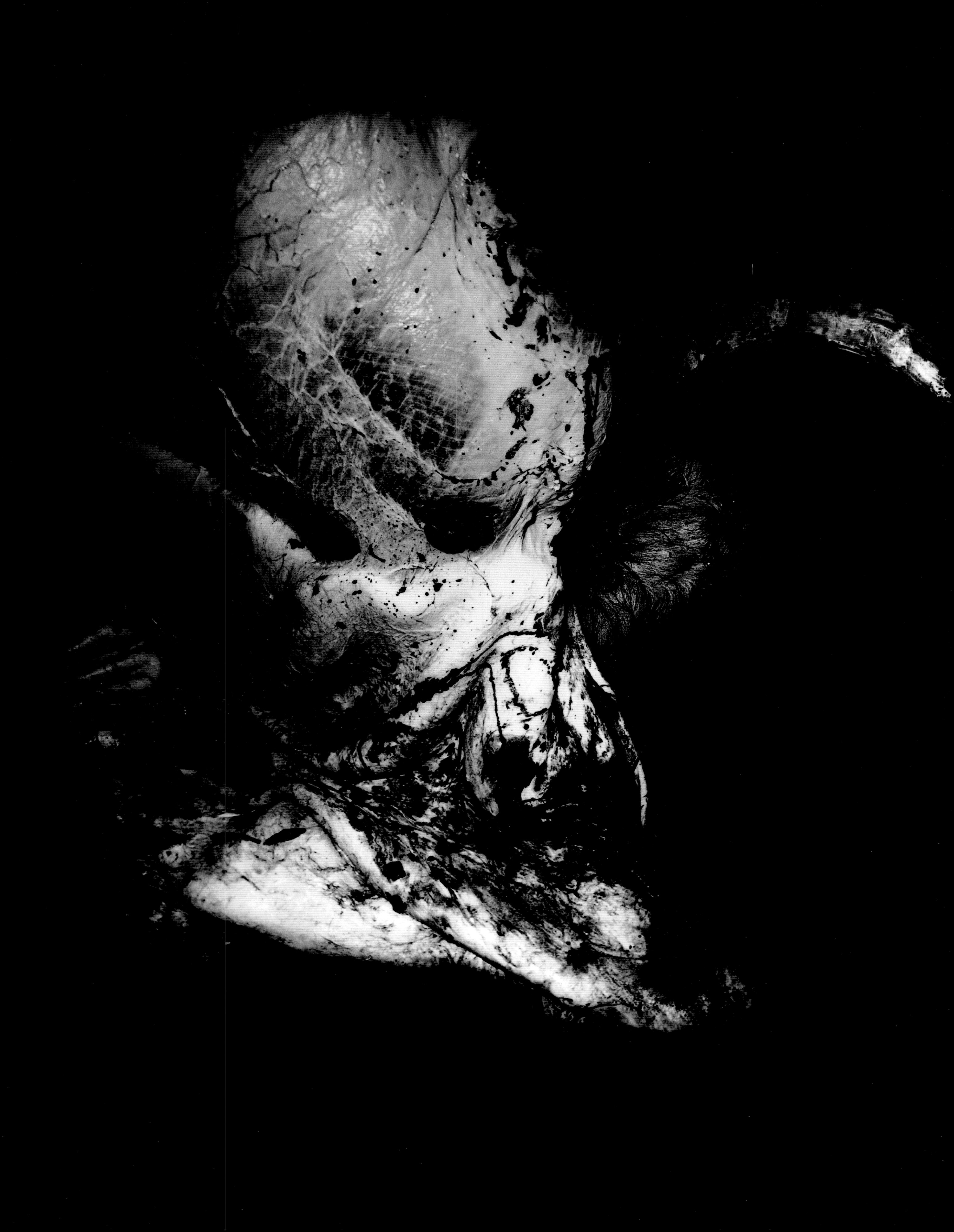

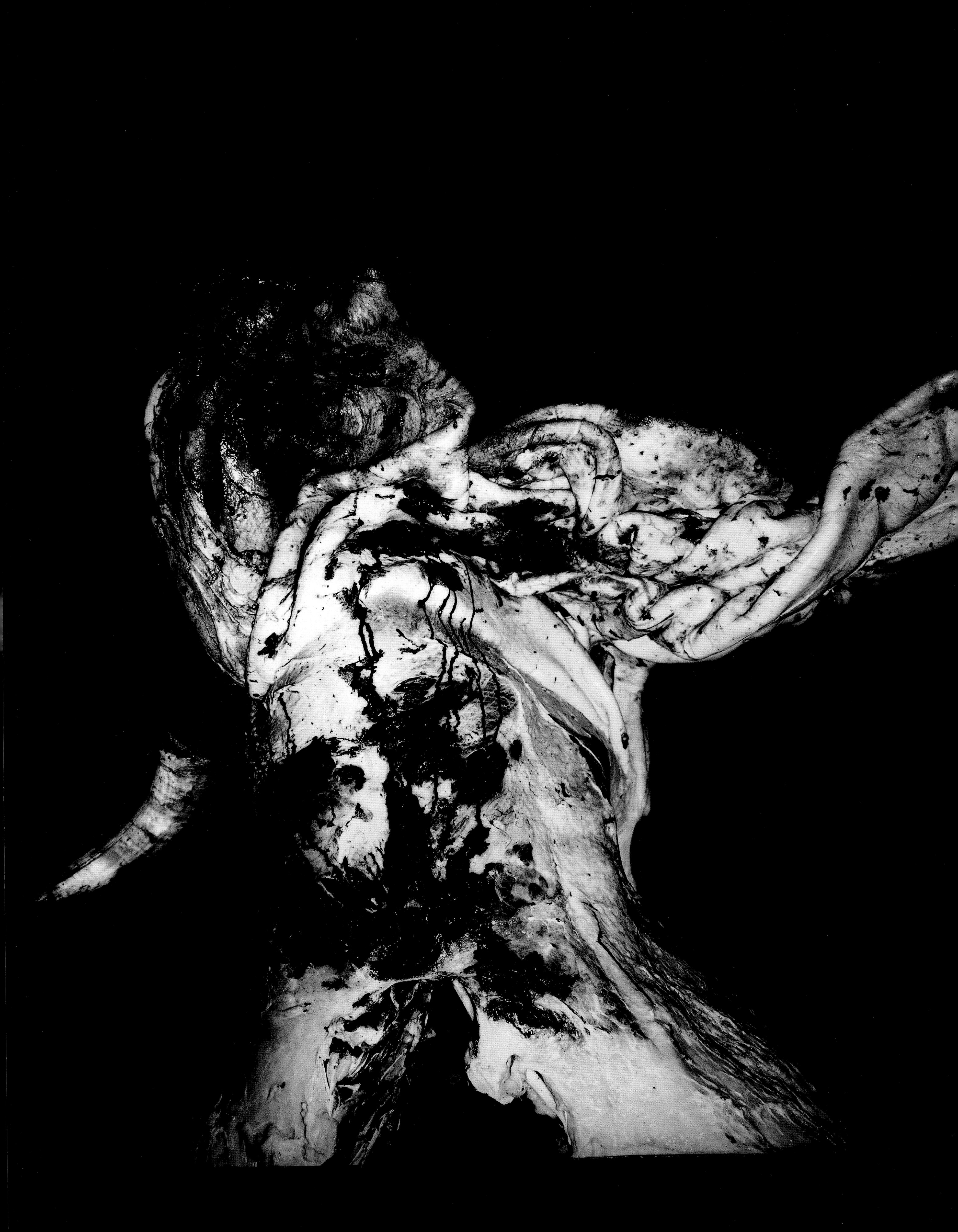

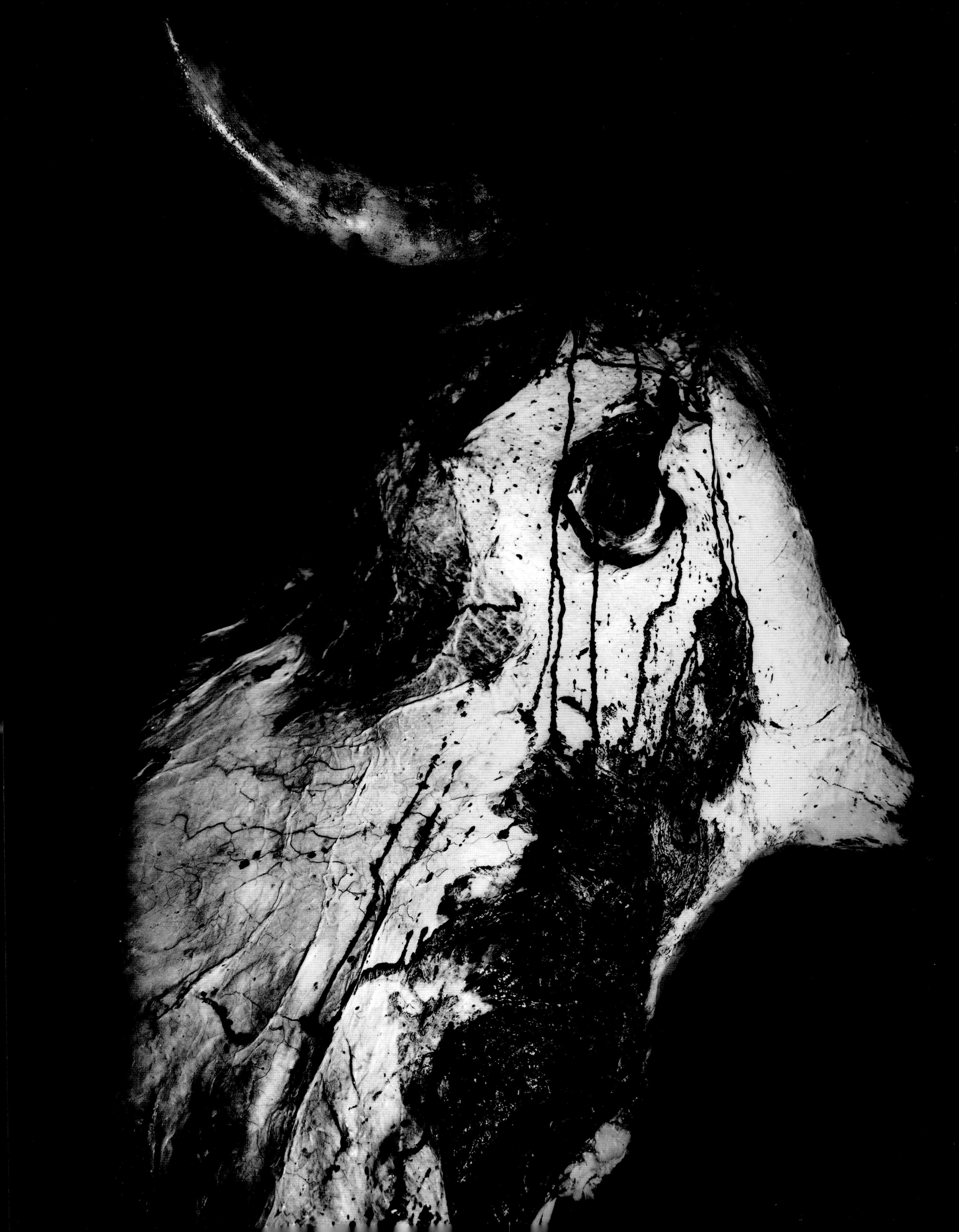

BIOGRAPHY

Touhami Ennadre was born on 18 February, 1953, at 208 rue Tnaker in the medina of Casablanca, Morocco, some time around midnight. His father was a butcher. In the butcher's shop where he worked, he met his employer's daughter, whom he married. His mother earned her living making rugs – beautiful rugs, hand-crafted beneath the sky of the medina. The third in a family of eight, Ennadre was strongly affected by the death of his brother Jamel-Eddine, who died at a very young age from measles: he still remembers his body decorated with ribbons, placed in the middle of the patio before being buried. Touhami himself benefitted from the medical services provided by French nuns from the "Mission Goutte de Lait", who vaccinated him, sparing him the premature death that was common at the time in the old working-class district of Casa. Childhood memories include the figure of Maria, a Spanish friend of his mother's who "always wore black, rather like a vicar". He received no religious upbringing in the Koran but remembers the mosque because he went there with his grandfather: "the toilets worked better there than any-where else". As a child, he only saw blood twice: once when a madman hit him over the head with a paving-stone; and on the day of his circumcision, which is performed at a late age among Arabs.

In 1961, his father was promised a job working in a foundry in Paris. Life being very hard in Morocco, the family made the great voyage, and the eight-year-old Ennadre saw snow for the first time, in Spain. The Ennadre family lived in a hotel in Epinay-sur-Seine and then in the chemin de Marville in the infernal shanty town of La Courneuve, where they spent several years before ending up at the Sonacotra hostel in the same Paris suburb. Through-out this entire period, Ennadre divided his time between the local primary school (a little) and football (a lot). His mother did everything she could to prevent him turning into a thug, a fate that threatened to befall him as it did all his companions in hard-ship. She bought him an organ, for he liked music. It didn't last, however, for it was too noisy for his father, whose gruelling work obliged him to sleep at odd hours. The genius of a mother's heart, how-ever, has more than one trick up its sleeve. She bought him his first camera, a Pentax "Spotmatic", so that he could make a start by photographing the family. The die were cast, Ennadre had hit on the lucky number; his life has since proved one long, painstaking confirmation of this motherly intuition.

He photographed tramps in the streets, his first hands on a trip to Morocco and then went to New York at the invitation of the photographer Roberto Salbitani. Salbitani's girl-friend, Julia Scully, who was the editor of the Modern Photography Magazine, owned a collection of photographs that impressed Ennadre and revealed a world to him, one where he would build his own world through sheer hard work and research. He would be a photographer. Not a reporter, but a photographer, a

BIOGRAPHIE

Touhami Ennadre est né le 18 février 1953, vers minuit, dans la médina de Casablanca, Maroc, au 208 de la rue Tnaker. Son père était boucher. Dans la boucherie où il travaillait, il rencontra la fille du patron, qu'il épousa. Sa mère gagnait sa vie en faisant des tapis. De beaux tapis, artisanalement ouvragés, sous le ciel de la médina.Troisième d'une famille de huit, Ennadre fut très impressionné par la mort de son frère Jamel-Eddine, emporté très jeune par la rougeole : il se rappelle encore ce corps enrubanné, posé au milieu du patio avant son ensevelissement. Touhami, quant à lui, bénéficia des services médicaux des religieuses françaises de la « Mission Goutte de lait » qui l'ont vacciné et lui ont évité la mort prématurée, habituelle à l'époque dans le vieux quartier populaire de Casa. Parmi quelques souvenirs d'enfance, le personnage de Maria, amie espagnole de sa mère, « toujours habillée de noir, un peu comme les curés ». Il ne bénéficia d'aucune éducation religieuse coranique et se souvient de la mosquée parce qu'il y allait avec son grand-père : « Les toilettes y fonctionnaient mieux qu'ailleurs ». Enfant, il ne vit le sang que deux fois : la première, lorsqu'un fou lui frappa le crâne avec un pavé, et le jour de sa circoncision, tardif chez les Arabes.

La vie étant économiquement très difficile au Maroc, en 1961, on promit à son père un travail à Paris, commme ouvrier dans une fonderie. La famille fit alors le grand voyage, et Ennadre, à huit ans, vit la neige pour la première fois, en Espagne. Les Ennadre habiteront sucessivement dans un hôtel à Epinay-sur-Seine et dans l'infernal bidonville de La Courneuve, chemin de Marville, où ils passeront plusieurs années avant d'aboutir au foyer Sonacotra de la même banlieue. Pendant toute cette période, Ennadre partage son temps entre l'école communale, un peu, et le football, beaucoup. Sa mère a tout tenté pour lui éviter la vie de loubard qui le menaçait comme tous ses camarades de galère. Elle lui acheta un orgue car il aimait la musique. Cela ne dura pas : trop de bruit pour le père que son dur travail contraignait à dormir à heures variables. Mais c'était ignorer que le génie d'une mère a plus d'un tour dans son cœur. Elle lui procura alors son premier appareil photographique, un Pentax « Spotmatic », afin qu'il puisse commencer en photographiant la famille. Les dés étaient jetés, Ennadre avait tiré le bon numéro ; sa vie ne sera qu'une longue et laborieuse confirmation de cette intuition maternelle.

Il photographia quelques clochards dans les rues, ses premières mains lors d'un voyage au Maroc et se rendit à New York à l'invitation du photographe Roberto Salbitani dont l'amie, Julia Scully, qui était éditeur du Modern Photography Magazine, possédait une collection d'archives photographiques qui

BIOGRAPHIE

Touhami Ennadre wurde am 18. Februar 1953 gegen Mitternacht in der Medina von Casablanca (Marokko), Rue Tnaker 208, geboren. Sein Vater war Metzger. In der Metzgerei, in der er arbeitete, begegnete der Vater der Tochter des Besitzers und heiratete sie. Touhamis Mutter verdiente ihren Lebensunterhalt am Webstuhl, unter dem Himmel der Medina, mit handwerklich schön gewirkten Teppichen. Der Tod seines Bruders, Jamel-Eddine, der noch als Kind an den Röteln starb, hat Ennadre, der das dritte von acht Kindern war, sehr getroffen: Er erinnert sich noch an den mit Bändern geschmückten Körper, wie er in der Mitte des Patio vor der Bestattung aufgebahrt war. Touhami hingegen erfuhr ärztliche Versorgung durch französische Nonnen der ›Mission Goutte de lait‹, die ihn geimpft und vor dem frühen Tod bewahrt haben, wie er zu jener Zeit im alten, volkstümlichen Viertel von Casablanca häufig vorkam. In einigen seiner Kindheitserinnerungen findet sich auch die Gestalt der Maria, einer spanischen Freundin seiner Mutter, die »immer schwarz gekleidet war, ein bißchen wie die Geistlichen«. Er wurde nicht im Koran unterwiesen und erinnert sich an die Moschee nur, weil er sie mit seinem Großvater aufsuchte: »Die Toiletten funktionierten dort besser als überall sonst.« Als Kind sah er nur zweimal Blut: Das erste Mal, als ein Verrückter ihm mit einem Pflasterstein auf den Schädel einschlug, und am Tag seiner Beschneidung, die bei den Arabern spät stattfindet.

Da das Leben in Marokko 1961 in wirtschaftlicher Hinsicht sehr schwierig war, nahm sein Vater in Paris ein Angebot als Arbeiter in einer Gießerei an. Folglich machte die Familie die weite Reise, und Ennadre sah mit acht Jahren zum ersten Mal in Spanien Schnee. Die Ennadres mußten zuerst in einem Hotel in Epinay-sur-Seine und dann im Elendsviertel von La Courneuve, Chemin de Marville, wohnen, wo sie mehrere Jahre verbringen sollten, bevor sie schließlich ins Foyer Sonacotra im gleichen Vorort kamen. In diesen Jahren verbringt Ennadre beim Fußball viel, in der Grundschule wenig Zeit. Seine Mutter versucht alles, damit er nicht zum Strolch wird, denn die Gefahr droht ihm wie allen seinen Kameraden in schwieriger Situation. Sie kauft ihm eine elektrische Orgel, weil er Musik mag. Die Freude war von kurzer Dauer, denn sein Vater, der durch seine harte Arbeit zu ganz verschiedenen Ruhezeiten gezwungen war, wurde dadurch gestört. Doch sollte man nicht verkennen, welchen Einfallsreichtum eine Mutter in ihrem Herzen bergen kann. Sie verschaffte ihm daraufhin seinen ersten Photoapparat, eine Pentax ›Spotmatic‹, damit er mit Aufnahmen von der Familie beginnen konnte. Die Würfel waren gefallen, Ennadre hatte die Glücksnummer gezogen. Seither ist sein Leben eine lange, arbeitsreiche Bestätigung dieses mütterlichen Einfalls.

Er photographierte einige Clochards auf den Straßen, seine ersten Hände anläßlich einer Reise nach Marokko, und er fuhr auf Einladung des Photographen Roberto Salbitani nach New York, wo dessen Freundin, Julia Scully, die das Modern Pho-

profession that needed to be built again and reinvented.

1976, 19 March: Death of Touhami Ennadre's mother from cancer.
Ennadre meets the photographer Regina Schmeken in Arles.
Ennadre receives the International Critics' Prize, which is awarded to Schmeken two years later.
Throughout this period, photography and travel are intimately related. Making shift as best he can, Ennadre can be found in Indonesia, Singapore, Malaysia, Thailand, Burma, Nepal and India. He also stays in Scandinavia and visits Spain, Portugal and Italy (first exhibition in Pisa).
Lives and exhibits his work at the Cité Internationale des Arts de la Ville de Paris, thanks to the unfailing kindness and friendship of its director, Mme Brunau.
1978: Michel Nuridsany invites him to take part in the exhibition "Tendances actuelles de la Photographie en France" at the ARC, at the Musée d'Art Moderne de la Ville de Paris, describing him in his catalogue as "the Van Gogh of photography". Jean-Luc Monterosso responds in *Le Quotidien de Paris* by calling him "Rimbaud the photographer".
That same year, Jean-Claude Lemagny, curator of the Cabinet des Estampes et des Photographies at the Bibliothèque Nationale in Paris, starts to show a keen interest in Ennadre's work, buying photographs for the library and also publishing them.
1982-85: United States, Canada, Germany, Morocco, Italy, Sicily.
1983: Françoise Elbaz and the painter André Elbaz introduce him to François Aubral, who has since given active expression to the affinities he feels with Ennadre's work.
1984: Awarded a one-year residence at the Villa Arson in Nice, whose president and director, Michel Butor and Henri Maccheroni, give him their warm support.
Comes to the attention of Michèle Chomette, who, in 1986, holds an exhibition of his work in her gallery in Paris.
1985-1987: Exhibition at the Karin Sachs Gallery in Munich.
1986: Granted French nationality.
1986-1993: Resumes travelling: Italy, Sicily, Portugal, Germany, Spain, New York, Japan, Morocco, Switzerland, Austria, Benin, Haiti, and Poland.
1987: Awarded the Young European Photographers Prize in Frankfurt.
1990: Major exhibition at the Institut du Monde Arabe in Paris.
1991: Meets Alain Jouffroy and, in 1992, collaborates on a book on Notre-Dame de Paris with him.
1995: A room is devoted to Ennadre's work at the exhibition "Vital: Three Contemporary African Artists" at the Tate Gallery in Liverpool. Nancy Spector writes the catalogue text, *Touhami Ennadre: The Trace of Time*.
Ennadre today divides his time between Paris, which he loves and where he lives, and his many journeys throughout the world.

impressionna Ennadre, lui découvrit un monde, celui où il devait, à force de recherches et de travail, construire son monde à lui. Il serait photographe. Pas reporter, mais photographe, un métier à reconstruire et à réinventer.

1976, 19 mars : mort de la mère de Touhami Ennadre, un cancer.
En 1976, il rencontre en Arles la photographe Regina Schmeken qui obtient le Prix international de la critique en 1978, deux ans après Ennadre, lauréat en 1976.
En ces années, l'aventure photographique et celle du voyage furent intimement mêlées. Avec les moyens du bord, on retrouve Ennadre en Indonésie, à Singapour, en Malaisie, en Thaïlande, en Birmanie, au Népal et en Inde. Il séjourne aussi en Scandinavie, va en Espagne, au Portugal et en Italie (première exposition à Pise).
Il habite et expose à la Cité Internationale des Arts de la Ville de Paris, grâce à la constante bienveillance et à l'amitié de Madame Brunau, sa directrice, qui ne lui feront jamais défaut.
En 1978, Michel Nuridsany lui ouvre les portes de « Tendances actuelles de la Photographie en France » à l'ARC, Musée d'Art Moderne de la Ville de Paris, et le traite de « Van Gogh de la photographie » dans son catalogue. A quoi Jean-Luc Monterosso répond par un « Rimbaud photographe » dans le *Quotidien de Paris*.
De 1982 à 1985, Etats-Unis, Canada, Allemagne, Maroc, Italie, Sicile.
Depuis 1978, Jean-Claude Lemagny, conservateur du Cabinet des Estampes et des photographies de la Bibliothèque Nationale, éprouve un vif intérêt pour l'œuvre d'Ennadre qu'il a édité et dont il a acheté des photographies pour la Bibliothèque Nationale.
En 1983, Françoise Elbaz et le peintre André Elbaz lui font rencontrer François Aubral qui, depuis, manifeste activement les affinités qu'il a avec cette œuvre.
Boursier pour une année à la villa Arson à Nice, en 1984, Michel Butor et Henri Maccheroni, respectivement président et directeur de la villa, lui apportent leur soutien chaleureux.
Michèle Chomette le repère en 1984 et l'expose dans sa galerie à Paris en 1986.
1985 et 1987 : exposition à la Galerie Karin Sachs à Munich.
En 1986, Ennadre obtient, à sa demande, la nationalité française par naturalisation.
Entre 1986 et 1993, il reprendra ses voyages : Italie, Sicile, Portugal, Allemagne, Espagne, New York, Japon, Maroc, Suisse, Autriche, Bénin, Haïti et Pologne.
En 1987, Ennadre est lauréat du Prix des jeunes photographes européens à Francfort.
En 1990, grande exposition à l'Institut du Monde arabe à Paris.
Il rencontre Alain Jouffroy en 1991 et fait un livre avec lui sur Notre-Dame de Paris en 1992.
En 1995, une salle lui est consacrée dans l'exposition « Vital. Three Contemporary African Artists » à la Tate Galerie de Liverpool.
Nancy Spector écrit le texte du catalogue : *Touhami Ennadre : The Trace of Time*.
Ennadre partage aujourd'hui son temps entre Paris, qu'il aime et où il réside, et ses nombreux voyages et séjours, ici ou là, à travers le monde.

tography Magazine herausgab, über reiche Photoarchive verfügte, die Ennadre beeindruckte und ihm eine Welt auftat, durch die er dank Recherchen und seiner Arbeit eine eigene Welt aufbauen sollte. Er sollte Photograph werden. Nicht Reporter, sondern Photograph, ein Beruf, den er neu schuf, neu erfand.

1976, 19. März: Die Mutter Touhami Ennadres stirbt an Krebs. In diesem Jahr begegnet er in Arles der Photographin Regina Schmeken, die 1978 den Internationalen Preis der Kritik erhielt, mit dem Ennadre 1976 ausgezeichnet worden war.
Zu dieser Zeit gehörten Photo- und Reiseabenteuer eng zusammen. Auf den mitgebrachten Photographien entdeckt man Ennadre in Indonesien, Singapur, Malaisia,Thailand, Birma, Nepal und Indien. Er hält sich auch in Skandinavien auf und fährt nach Portugal und Italien (erste Ausstellung in Pisa).
Dank des immerwährenden Wohlwollens und der Freundschaft mit Madame Brunau, der Leiterin der Cité Internationale des Arts in Paris, wohnt und stellt er dort aus.
1978 öffnet ihm Michel Nuridsany die Tore zur ›Tendances actuelles de la Photographie en France‹ im ARC, Musée d'Art Moderne de la Ville de Paris, und spricht in seinem Katalog von ihm als dem »Van Gogh der Photographie« - worauf Jean-Luc Monterosso ihn im *Quotidien de Paris* »Rimbaud als Photograph« nennt.
Von 1982 bis 1985 unternimmt Ennadre Reisen in die Vereinigten Staaten, nach Kanada, Deutschland, Marokko, Italien, Sizilien.
Seit 1978 zeigt Jean-Claude Lemagny, Konservator der Graphischen Sammlung und zuständig für Photographie in der Bibliothèque Nationale in Paris, Interesse am Werk Ennadres, von dem er Photographien für die Bibliothèque Nationale gekauft hat.
1983 bringen ihn Françoise Elbaz und der Maler André Elbaz mit François Aubral zusammen, der seither seiner Beziehung, die er zu diesem Werk hat, rege Ausdruck verleiht. Als Ennadre 1984 ein Jahresstipendium für die Villa Arson in Nizza erhält, weiß er sich von Michel Butor, dem Präsidenten, und Henri Maccheroni, dem Leiter der Villa, unterstützt.
1984 wird Michèle Chomette auf ihn aufmerksam und stellt 1986 in ihrer Pariser Galerie Arbeiten von ihm aus.
1985, 1987: Ausstellung in der Galerie Karin Sachs in München.
1986 erhält er die französische Staatsbürgerschaft.
Zwischen 1986 und 1993 unternimmt er wieder zahlreiche Reisen: Italien, Sizilien, Portugal, Deutschland, Spanien, New York, Japan, Marokko, Schweiz, Österreich, Bénin, Haiti und Polen.
1987 erhält Ennadre in Frankfurt den Preis der jungen europäischen Photographen.
1990: große Ausstellung im Institut du Monde arabe in Paris.
1991 begegnet er Alain Jouffroy und macht 1992 ein Buch mit ihm über Notre-Dame von Paris.
1995 erhält er einen Saal in der Ausstellung ›Vital. Three Contemporary African Artists‹ in der Tate Gallery, Liverpool. Nancy Spector verfaßt einen Katalogtext unter dem Titel *Touhami Ennadre: The Trace of Time*.
Touhami Ennadre verbringt heute seine Zeit zwischen Paris, das er liebt, wo er wohnt, und zahlreichen Reisen und Aufenthalten vielerorts in der ganzen Welt.

EXHIBITIONS, PUBLICATIONS, AND AWARDS

SOLO EXHIBITIONS EXPOSITIONS PERSONNELLES
EINZELAUSSTELLUNGEN

1977 Galleria Nadar, Pisa.
1982 Private exhibition, New York.
1984 Cité Internationale des Arts, Paris.
1985 Présence artistique du Maroc, Maison de la Culture, Grenoble.
Photographies du corps humain, Musée Fabre, Montpellier.
Galerie Karin Sachs, Munich.
1986 La Mort vive, Galerie Michèle Chomette, Paris.
Foire Internationale de l'Art Contemporain (FIAC), Grand Palais, Paris.
1987 Galerie l'Atelier, Rabat.
Galerie Karin Sachs, Munich.
1990 Retrospective: Oeuvres Photographiques 1980-1990, Institut du Monde arabe, Paris.
International festival, Coïmbra.
1991 Institut français, Athens.
1993 Notre-Dame de Paris, FNAC et Caisse Nationale des Monuments Historiques et des Sites, FNAC-Forum, Paris.
15th festival of photography, Trégor/Lannion (Brittany).
1994 Exit Art, 548 Broadway, New York.
1996 Nederlands Fotoinstituut, Rotterdam.
Touhami Ennadre - Lumière noire, Dany Keller Galerie, Munich.
Herculaneum, Staatliche Antikensammlungen, Glyptothek, Munich

GROUP EXHIBITIONS EXPOSITIONS COLLECTIVES
GRUPPENAUSSTELLUNGEN

1977 Tendances actuelles de la Photographie en France, ARC, Musée d'Art Moderne de la Ville de Paris, Paris.
1979-84 Cité Internationale des Arts, Paris.
1985 Das Aktfoto, Museum für moderne Kunst, Vienna; Frankfurter Kunstverein, Frankfurt am Main; Museum für Kunst und Kulturgeschichte der Stadt Dortmund, Dortmund.
La photographie créative, Bibliothèque Nationale, Pavillon des Arts, Paris.
Regards sur la Villa Arson, Centre National d'Art Contemporain, Nice.
1986 Des photographies dans le tableau, Art Jonction International, Nice.
Sélection Michèle Chomette et Commanderie Sainte Luce/RIO, Arles.
Rencontres internationales d'Arles, Arles.
Intensités nomades, Musée Fabre, Montpellier.
1987 Intensités nomades, Galerie d'Exposition de la Direction des Musées, Bab-er-Rouah, Rabat; Centre d'Art Vivant, Tunis.
Mémoires de l'origine, des photographes en Méditerrannée, Centre de la Vieille Charité, Marseille.
La Création au sud, Art Jonction International, Nice.
Baroques photographiques, Abbaye-aux-Dames, Saintes/Chambre Claire, Paris.
Junge Europäische Photographen/87, Frankfurter Kunstverein, Frankfurt am Main.
1988 Baroques photographiques, Musée Cantini, Centre de la Vieille Charité, Marseille; Cercle municipal, Luxembourg, and Centre Culturel Vaudreuil/Jean Gagnant, Limoges.
Propositions pour une collection de photographies, Art Jonction International, Nice.
Splendeurs et misères du corps, Musée d'art et d'histoire, Fribourg, Switzerland, and the Musée d'Art Moderne de la Ville de Paris.
Bilder der Vergänglichkeit, Internationale Photoszene Köln, Institut français, Cologne.
1989 Photographie en liberté: la photographie française, Fundação Gulbenkian, Lisbon, and Frankfurter Kunstverein, Frankfurt am Main.
1991 Cité Internationale des Arts: 25ème anniversaire, Paris.
Photographie en liberté, New York / Mexico / Kawasaki / Tokyo
1992 In vitro, Fundación Joan Miró, Barcelona.
Traces, Musée des Beaux-Arts, Angoulême, France.
Transvoice, American Center, Paris, and Whitney Museum of American Art, New York.
Multimedia project with posters in the New York subway and Paris Metro, Centre Georges Pompidou, Paris.
Images Métisses, Institut du Monde arabe, Paris.
Cité Internationale des Arts, Paris.
1993 Große Kunstausstellung München, Haus der Kunst, Munich.
V Biennale internazionale delle photographie, Museo dell'Automobile Carlo Biscaretti di Ruffia, Turin.
Cité Internationale des Arts, Paris.
1994 Le Corps en scène, Institut français, Madrid.
10th European Photographic Exhibition, Bad Homburg v. d. H., Germany.
1995 Vital: Three Contemporary African Artists, Tate Gallery Liverpool, Liverpool.
Die Rote Burg. Zehn künstlerische Positionen zur Alhambra, Haus der Kulturen der Welt, Berlin.
1996 African photography. A triptych, Solomon R. Guggenheim Museum, New York.
Collection in Context. Selected photographs from the collection of Henry Buhl, 4th Annual SoHo Partnership Benefit, Thread Waxing Space, New York 1996.

Michel Nuridsany, "Tendances actuelles de la photographie en France", in exhibition catalogue ARC 2, Musée d'Art Moderne de la Ville de Paris, 1977.

Jean-Luc Monterosso, "La jeune photographie française sort enfin du ghetto", in Le Quotidien de Paris, 25 November 1977.

François Aubral, in exhibition catalogue Photographie, Cité Internationale des Arts, Paris 1984.

Jean-Claude Lemagny, "La Photographie créative", in exhibition cataloge, Bibliothèque Nationale, Pavillon des Arts, Paris 1985.

Exhibition catalogue "Présence artistique au Maroc", Maison de la Culture, Grenoble 1985.

Exhibition catalogue "Photographs of the Human Body", Journées Internationales de Montpellier, Montpellier 1985.

Bauret, Gabriel, "Touhami Ennadre", in *Camera International* no. 5, Paris 1985.

Christian Gattinoni, "La photo saisie par la mort", in *Canal,* 1986, p. 43-44.

Patrick Roegiers, "La Mort Vive de Touhami Ennadre", in *Le Monde,* 16/17 March 1986, p. 9.

Christine Buci-Glucksmann, in exhibition catalogue "Intensités nomades", Musée Fabre, Montpellier 1986.

Exhibition catalogue Foire International d'Art Contemporain (FIAC), Grand Palais, Paris 1986.

Exhibition catalogue "Mémoire de l'origine des photographes en Méditerrannée", Centre de la Vieille Charité, Marseille 1987.

Exhibition catalogue "Junge Europäische Photographen/87", Frankfurter Kunstverein, Frankfurt am Main 1987.

Umberto Pappalardo, "Requiem aeternam, Pompeii", in *Archeologia viva,* Florence 1987.

François Aubral, in exhibition catalogue "L'Art contemporain arabe", Institut du Monde arabe, Paris 1987.

Philippe Gardenal, in *Libération,* 9 November 1988, p. 40.

François Aubral, "Touhami Ennadre", in exhibition catalogue 9th Photographic Meeting, Coïmbra 1988.

Frédéric Pajac, "Un cri", in *Voir,* 1988, p. 35-37.

Evelyn Schels, "Photographische Skulpturen", in *Süddeutsche Zeitung,* 17/18 November 1990, p. 16.

Bruno Gosset, in *Le Quotidien de Paris,* 1990.

Kadhim Jihad, in *Al Youm Sebaa,* 1990, p. 41.

Jean-Louis Poitevin, "Brûler la nuit", in *Kanal,* no. 12/13, February/March 1991.

Alain Jouffroy, in exhibition catalogue "Touhami Ennadre", Institut français, Athens 1991.

Exhibition catalogue Cité Internationale des Arts: 25ème anniversaire, Paris 1991.

Minato Chihiro, in *The Sun,* Tokyo, no. 365, November 1991, p. 157-165.

François Aubral, "Lumière noire", in *Déjà-vu,* Tokyo, no. 12, April 1993.

Paolo Bianchi, "Touhami Ennadre", in *Kunstforum International* 122, 1993, p. 259-261.

Evelyn Schels, "Die Hände der Welt", in *Süddeutsche Zeitung,* 19 October 1993, p. 13.

Süddeutsche Zeitung, March-April 1994, (SZ-Edition).

Pivin, Jean-Loup, "Touhami Ennadre", in *Revue noire* no. 12, March-May 1994, Paris.

Heiner Henninges, "Touhami Ennadre: Schwarzes Licht", in *Schwarzweiss* no. 4, September 1994, p. 27-34.

Alain Jouffroy, "Cet instant-là, le 24 août de l'an 79", rubrique L'Œil Naïf de Régis Debray, in *Libération Magazine,* 21 January 1995.

Alfons Hug u. a., "Die Rote Burg". Zehn künstlerische Positionen zur Alhambra, exhibition catalogue, Haus der Kulturen der Welt, Berlin, Milan 1995.

Nancy Spector, "Touhami Ennadre: The Trace of Time", in exhibition catalogue Vital: Three Contemporary African Artists, Tate Gallery Liverpool, Liverpool 1995.

Kathryn Marx "Touhami Ennadre, L'ivresse du noir" in: *Photographies Magazine,* June 1996, p. 88

Süddeutsche Zeitung, August 1996 (SZ-Edition)

Thierry Chervel, "Photos, um kein Bild zu machen", in *Süddeutsche Zeitung,* 13 August 1996, S. 11.

AWARDS DISTINCTIONS PREISE

Prix international de la critique, Arles, 1976.

Villa Arson scholarship, CNAC, Nice, 1984.

Young European Photography Award, Frankfurt am Main, 1987.

Villa Médicis Hors les Murs award, Paris 1991.

Leonardo da Vinci prize, presented by the French Ministry of Foreign Affairs, Paris 1993.

UNESCO Aschberg grant: Fondation Afrique en création, 1995.

RESURRECTION

RÉSURRECTION

AUFERSTEHUNG

1988